FOOTBALL MADE SIMPLE: A SPECTATOR'S GUIDE

FOURTH EDITION

by Dave Ominsky and P.J. Harari

Illustrations by Stephen J. Lattimer

Cover Design by Eugene Cheltenham

Hand Signals by Anna Mendoza

Photographs © by
Allsport Photography and Bruce Bennett Studios

2006 Reprint
© 2002, 1998, 1997, 1994 First Base Sports, Inc.,
Los Angeles, California

http://www.firstbasesports.com

Look for these other Spectator Guides:
- Basketball Made Simple
- Ice Hockey Made Simple
- Soccer Made Simple

2006 Reprint
© 2002, 1998, 1997, 1994 First Base Sports, Inc.,
Los Angeles, California

ISBN-13: 978-1-884309-12-0
ISBN-10: 1-884309-12-7
Library of Congress Catalog Card Number: 2002091853

We welcome your comments and questions:
FIRST BASE SPORTS, INC.
P.O. BOX 1731
MANHATTAN BEACH, CALIFORNIA 90267-1731
U.S.A.
E-mail: feedback@firstbasesports.com

Typesetting by Jelico Graphics

HOW TO USE THIS BOOK

Americans truly love to watch football — over 60% watch the game at some level, whether it be high school, college or professional. Football is also exploding in popularity overseas in countries such as England and Japan. Yet millions of potential fans still feel left out of the excitement because they think the game is too complicated for them to understand.

This book aims to educate anyone who wants to know more about this exciting game. It is written to be used by a variety of audiences — adults who want to become fans, children who need a solid grounding in the basics of the sport they are playing and even existing fans who want a quick reference guide to their favorite sport.

Each chapter has been written to stand alone, so you do not have to sit and read the book from cover to cover. However, the chapters do build on each other, so if you start at page 1 and read through to the end, the chapters flow logically and gradually become more detailed as you progress.

This book will mainly treat football as it is played at the professional and collegiate levels, although the main principles of the sport are the same even at the high school level and below. Rules presented in this guide are interpreted from the Official Playing Rules of the National Football League (NFL). Information from the NCAA Football Rules and Interpretations is added when college rules differ significantly from the NFL's.

To help the reader, rules as well as any word or phrase printed in *italics* can be referenced quickly and easily using the book's glossary or index. So get ready to learn about football, the sport that has attracted such a loyal following, and you too can experience its fun and excitement.

FOOTBALL ORGANIZATIONS

Four main football organizations exist to govern the game in North America and overseas:

NFL (National Football League)
Established in 1922, the *NFL* is the major outdoor professional football league in the United States. Its 32 teams play a 16-game season from early September through late December. This is followed by *playoffs* and the *Super Bowl*, the league's championship played each January. The NFL is headquartered in New York and has developed its own official set of rules.

NCAA (National Collegiate Athletic Association)
Originally established in 1910 as the rules committee for the emerging game of football, this organization now governs dozens of other collegiate sports. The *NCAA* determines the guidelines players must follow to be eligible to play collegiate sports, and its Football Rules Committee maintains playing rules that differ only slightly from the NFL's. The NCAA is based in Overland Park, Kansas.

CFL (Canadian Football League)
This 8-team Canadian professional league plays an 18-game season that begins in late June and climaxes in November with the *Grey Cup*, the league championship. CFL rules differ from the NFL's. For example, the *field* is longer and wider (150 x 65 yards), each team plays with 1 more player (12 per side) and teams only get 3 *downs* (1 fewer than the NFL) to make 10 yards. Also Canadian team rosters can hold only 39 players, far fewer than the NFL's 53, and must limit the number of non-Canadian "import" players to a maximum of 20. The CFL is based in Toronto.

NFL Europe
Called the *World League of American Football* when created in 1991, this league was suspended after two seasons until 1995 when it was resurrected as an all-European league to take advantage of the NFL's popularity in Europe. It was renamed NFL Europe in 1998. The league consists of six teams located throughout Europe (Amsterdam, Barcelona, Berlin, Dusseldorf, Frankfort and Scotland), and its 10-game season begins in April and culminates with the World Bowl in late June. Teams are comprised largely of American players, but are required to carry a minimum of 8 non-North Americans.

TABLE OF CONTENTS

THE ORIGINS OF FOOTBALL

THE BEGINNING

The game of football as we know it today evolved from *soccer* during the 19th Century. A kicking game played by man for thousands of years, soccer was eventually transformed by a faction of American college students who wanted to make their version of the game more fun. This evolution actually began in England in 1823, when during a soccer match, William Ellis, a student at Rugby, became frustrated by his inability to advance the ball with his feet, so he picked it up and ran with it. While clearly against the rules of soccer, some players liked the idea of carrying the ball, and the sport of *rugby* was born.

The worldwide popularity of rugby increased during the 1800s, spreading to colleges in the northeastern United States by the mid-1800s. In 1876, representatives from Harvard and Yale, two schools that favored rugby over soccer, met in Massachusetts to formalize their own set of guidelines for a kicking game, and adopted rules similar to those that governed rugby in England. They called their new game football, played with an oval-shaped ball rather than a round soccer ball, and called the new governing organization the *Intercollegiate Football Association* (IFA).

Between 1880 and 1883, one of Yale's players convinced the IFA Rules Committee to enact a series of new rules that created a game similar to the football played in America today. His name was *Walter Camp*, and many historians consider him the father of modern football.

THE NFL IS BORN

As football continued to evolve in the university setting during the early-1900s, the first professional teams emerged. They played using collegiate rules established by the newly-formed *National Collegiate Athletic Association* (*NCAA*). In 1920, organizers from 11 teams met in Canton, Ohio to form a stable professional league called the *American Professional*

Football Association (*APFA*). By 1922, the league had adopted its own set of rules and renamed itself the *National Football League* (*NFL*).

THE 1920s and 1930s
The popularity of football began to climb in the 1920s. In 1925, the NFL's Chicago Bears signed Harold (Red) Grange, an extremely popular *All-American halfback* from the University of Illinois, to play for them. With their new college star, the Bears attracted the largest football crowds yet, drawing about 75,000 fans as the visiting team in games against the New York Giants and the Los Angeles Tigers. In 1933, the NFL was split into two *divisions*, and the first NFL championship game was played between the two division winners, the Bears and the Giants.

THE MERGER
As football gained more exposure, various leagues emerged to compete with the NFL. By the 1950s, 4 leagues had tried but none survived more than 4 years. It was not until 1960 that another professional league was strong enough to coexist with the NFL — this was the *American Football League* (*AFL*), an 8-team league established by millionaire Lamar Hunt. Over the next several years, the two leagues competed for college *draft choices* and lucrative television contracts, and though the NFL got better deals, the AFL held its own.

Finally, in 1966, leaders of the two leagues agreed that in 1970, they would merge into a single league under the NFL name and split into two *conferences* that would play one another — the *American Football Conference* (*AFC*), consisting of AFL teams, and the *National Football Conference* (*NFC*), containing the original NFL teams. The leagues also agreed that in 1967, prior to the full merger, they would begin acquiring young players in a single college draft and would play the first Championship Game between NFL and AFL Champions. This game later became known as the *Super Bowl*.

Many believed that the AFL was inferior and that its teams would not be competitive with NFL teams in the newly merged league, but the AFL proved it was worthy even before the official merger. In 1969, the AFL's New York Jets, led by a brash young quarterback named *Joe Namath*, defeated the heavily-favored Baltimore Colts in Super Bowl III to earn the AFL its first championship.

THE MODERN GAME: POPULARITY SOARS

The merger of the NFL and AFL helped generate even greater interest in football, and during the 1970s, it even surpassed baseball, "America's pastime," as the country's favorite sport. The prevalence of televised football greatly contributed to the rise of the sport, as at least 3 games were shown on the major networks each week, including the first football action shown in prime time — ABC's *Monday Night Football* (started in 1970). In 1986, the telecast of Super Bowl XX was watched by 127 million viewers, surpassing the final episode of M*A*S*H as the most-watched television show in history. The league set new attendance records nearly every year during the 1980s and 1990s, with games averaging well over 60,000 fans during that period.

Along with this explosive fan interest has come tremendous monetary rewards for teams and players. Television rights paid to professional football leagues have grown from around $25 million per year before the merger to over $2 billion today. The increase in player salaries has been just as dramatic.

To the league's credit, it has continued to make changes in the rules to maintain football's burgeoning popularity. For example, the *passing* game was given a boost in the 1970s by making it easier for *offensive linemen* to *pass block* and by placing more restrictions on *defensive backs* when guarding pass *receivers*. The trend of favoring exciting offensive football was continued in 1994 with the adoption of the 2-*point conversion* and rules that discourage long *field goal attempts*. The continued evolution of football is actually a part of the game, a trend started when a few young Americans wanted to make the game they were playing more fun.

OBJECT OF THE GAME

Football is a territorial battle played on a *field* between two teams of 11 players each. Each team tries to move a ball by running with it and throwing it among themselves, trying to get near its opponent's end of the  field where it can earn *points* by *scoring* a *touchdown* or a *field goal*. The object of the game is to win by scoring more points than the other team.

Football is exciting because it combines the incredible skills of the world's finest athletes with the intricate strategy of a war. Huge mountains of men collide in brutal head-on clashes to make room for lightning-quick runners who dash down the field with the ball. Other players hurl the ball 50 yards with perfect accuracy to agile teammates who leap, twist and dive to snare the ball into their clutches. All of this is orchestrated by *coaches*, who plan every movement of the players to gain an advantage. The opposing coaches try to do the same. These are the elements that make football such an entertaining sport to watch.

The rules and strategies of football are among the most complex of any sport, yet the game can be understood and enjoyed quite easily at a basic level without becoming lost in too much detail. Most of the rules are quite logical, designed to reward physical play and smart strategy while protecting players from serious injury. If you keep these two ideas in mind while reviewing the chapters of this guide, you will have little trouble understanding the game of football.

THE FOOTBALL FIELD

A football game is played on a large rectangular *field* covered with either a grass or *Astroturf* surface. Each team defends one end of the field by trying to prevent its opponent from moving a ball towards that end. The field is a total of 120 yards long and 53 ¹/₃ yards (160 feet) wide bounded on all 4 sides by a thick white border at least 6 feet wide called the *boundary line*. (See **Figure 1**) Along the length of the field this line is called the *sideline* and at each end of the field it is the *end line*. Whenever the ball, or a player holding it, touches or crosses over one of these lines, he is said to be *out of bounds* or outside the "field of play." Inside these lines, the ball is said to be *in bounds*.

At each end of the field, the following are found:

Goal Line — This 8-inch wide line runs parallel to each end line, 10 yards into the field of play. When a team with the ball crosses the goal line and enters the *end zone* defended by its opponent, it scores a *touchdown* or *2-point conversion* and is awarded *points*.

End Zone — This is the area between the end line and goal line which a team "on *offense*" tries to enter to score. A short orange *pylon* stands vertically at each of the end zone's 4 corners. The ground inside most end zones is usually painted with the name of the home team or some other colorful design.

Goalpost — This tall metallic structure stands at the back of each end zone. It consists of a *crossbar* and two *uprights* that extend upward from it, supported directly above the end line by a base. (See **Figure 2**) Teams try to kick the ball above the crossbar and between the uprights to score a *field goal* or *extra point*. The base is padded to protect players who might accidentally collide with it.

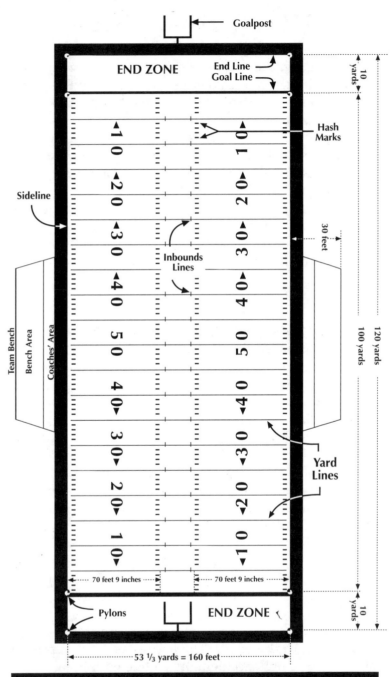

Figure 1: A football field.

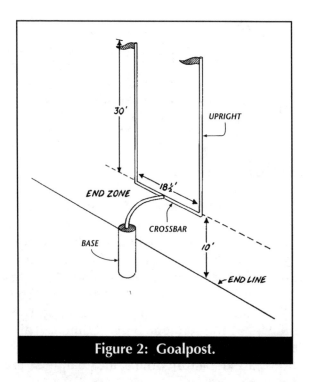

Figure 2: Goalpost.

Across the entire field, the following lines are painted:

Yard Lines — To keep track of the movement made by each team, the length of the field is divided by marks called yard lines. A yard line is named after its distance from the nearest goal line (e.g., the 20-yard line is 20 yards from the nearest goal line).

Hash Marks — These short yard lines near the center of the field define the area where all plays must start. They are located 70 feet 9 inches in bounds from each sideline (60 feet in college). In order to keep the teams near the center of the field, no *play* can be started between a hash mark and its closest sideline, an area known as a *side zone*. If a play ends in one of the side zones, the ball is placed at the adjacent hash mark for the next play.

PLAYER BENCHES

When players are not on the field, they retreat to their team's *bench area* behind the sidelines where they can sit and rest. During the game, only coaches may stand within 6 feet of the sideline, in an area known as the *coaches' area*. The bench areas of the two teams are usually on opposite sides of the field.

WHOSE SIDE IS WHOSE?

In war, a country's *territory* is that land which it occupies and defends. The situation is similar in football, where a team's territory is considered to be the area that it defends. This is why the end of the field a team is defending (has its back to) is called its "own end," the goal line in that half of the field is its "own goal line" and a 20-yard line in its own end is called its "own 20-yard line." You might also hear an announcer say something like, "The Eagles have the ball at the Raiders' 33-yard line." This means that the next play will start 33 yards from the goal line the Raiders are defending, the same goal line the Eagles are attacking.

THE RED ZONE

When a team has the ball deep in enemy territory, "inside" the opponent's 20-yard line (between it and the goal line), it is often said to be in the *"red zone."* In this area, every play is critical since a team can more easily score a touchdown or field goal from this position so close to the goal line.

UNIFORMS & EQUIPMENT

THE FOOTBALL

A *football* is an inflated rubber bladder enclosed in a pebble-grained leather cover. White laces are sewn on the tan-colored surface to help players grip the football when throwing it. Unlike balls used in most sports, a football is not a sphere but is elongated in one direction, and this affects the game in a couple of important ways. The ball's uneven shape often causes it to bounce unpredictably, so players trying to control it prefer not to let it hit the ground. Second, to throw a football accurately and with distance, a player must impart a spin to keep the ball pointed in the same direction while in flight, called a *spiral* (explained further in **PLAYER SKILLS**).

Different-sized balls are used at different levels of play — younger children play with smaller footballs. In the *NFL*, the ball must be a Wilson™ brand with dimensions shown in **Figure 3** and a weight of 14-15 ounces. College rules do not require any specific brand of football, and the required measurements are only slightly different from the NFL's.

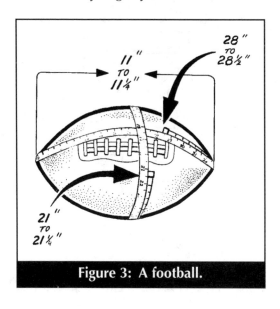

Figure 3: A football.

PLAYER EQUIPMENT

Because of the violent body contact involved in football, players wear several pounds of padding and other protective gear to help prevent serious injuries. (See **Figure 4**) To protect them from head injuries, all players must wear a *helmet* with foam-rubber padding inside secured to their heads by a *chin strap*. Inflatable liners have recently been added for extra protection and a snugger fit. The logo of a player's team is usually printed on both sides of his helmet. A *facemask* made of plastic-coated steel bars is attached to the front of the helmet to protect players from being hit in the face. A clear plastic face shield is optional. A *mouthpiece* used to protect players' teeth and lips is what you might see hanging out of their mouths between plays.

Other equipment includes *shoulder pads* (a single protective piece that protects the shoulders and upper rib cage), knee pads, elbow pads, hip pads and thigh pads. All of these

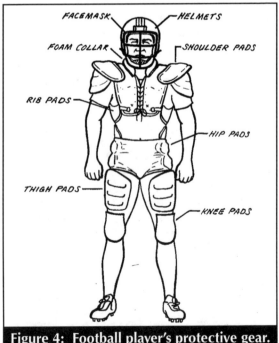

Figure 4: Football player's protective gear.

pads fit between the player and his uniform. Of these pads, *kickers* are only required to wear the shoulder pads. Players also use liberal amounts of tape wrapped around ankle, wrist and knee joints to prevent sprains and dislocations.

Shoes are critical equipment for football players, and the type chosen often varies with the type of playing surface. On grass, players wear shoes with *cleats* to dig into the soil to give them traction, while on *Astroturf*, players use special shoes that provide better grip on an artificial surface. On any surface, players are prohibited from wearing cleats that come to a sharp point. Some kickers wear no shoe at all on their kicking foot.

PLAYER UNIFORMS
Players wear pants and a *jersey* that must be tucked in to cover all protective padding. Each NFL team has two jerseys — a white one, and one in its official team color. Prior to its first game, each team chooses which of these it will wear at *home games* for the entire season. If it chooses its team color, each *visiting team* will wear its white jersey; if it chooses white, each visiting team will wear its own team color. On each player's jersey are printed his name and number large enough so that fans and *officials* can identify him from far away.

Each player's uniform number must match the position he plays on the field according to the following chart (each of these players will be discussed in the chapter on **PLAYER POSITIONS**):

Player Position	Uniform Number
quarterback, punter, place kicker	1-19
running back, defensive back	20-49
center	50-59 (or 60-79 if needed)
linebacker	50-59 (or 90-99 if needed)
offensive guard, tackle	60-79
defensive lineman	60-79 (or 90-99 if needed)
wide receiver, tight end	80-89 (or 10-19 if needed)

We will now see **HOW THE GAME IS PLAYED**.

HOW THE GAME IS PLAYED

There is more to football than uniformed men running around and hitting each other. It is a game governed by an elaborate set of rules that dictate a definite sequence of events throughout the game. Football follows a rhythm, with action starting and stopping in spurts called *plays*. Everything important in football occurs during a play — the team with the ball can advance with it, get pushed backwards, lose it to the other team or score. Between plays, participants rest and plan their strategies for the next play. We begin by looking at the basic confrontation in football — the 11 players of the offense against the 11 players of the defense.

OFFENSE VS. DEFENSE

At the start of a play, the team holding the ball has *possession* of it and is called the *offense* or *offensive team* (it is "on offense"). It uses *running plays* and *passing plays* to try to advance the ball towards the opposition's *goal line* and across it (a *touchdown*), or to kick it through the *uprights* of the *goalpost* (a *field goal*). The series of plays a team puts together while it maintains possession is called a *drive*, and the location on the field that an offense has reached is known as its *field position*. The best field position for a team is near its opponent's goal line, while the worst field position is close to its own goal line.

The team that does not have the ball is called the *defense* or *defensive team* (it is *on defense*). It tries to prevent the offense from scoring by *tackling* the player with the ball or forcing him *out of bounds* to minimize his advance. The ball can *change possession* from one team to the other in several different ways (explained later in this chapter), with the offensive team becoming the defense, and the defensive team becoming the offense. Since offense and defense are played by different sets of players on a team, whenever there is a change of possession, all the players on the field need to be replaced. When neither team controls the ball, such as when it is bouncing around on the field, it is called a *loose ball* and can be picked up by either team which then becomes the offense on the next play.

SCORING

There are 5 ways for teams to score points, and they are discussed in detail in the next chapter entitled **SCORING**:

Type of Score	Points
Touchdown	6
Field Goal	3
Safety	2
2-point Conversion	2
Point-After-Touchdown (extra point)	1

DOWNS: CHANCES FOR TEAM TO ADVANCE BALL

When a team is on offense, it is given 4 chances to advance the ball 10 yards or it loses possession. Each of these opportunities is called a *down*, and the 4 downs together are a *series* or *set of downs*. As soon as the ball is advanced 10 or more yards, past an imaginary line called the *necessary line*, the team is immediately given a new set of downs, or 4 new opportunities to get 10 more yards from the ball's new location. This is called achieving a *first down*. When a team first gets possession of the ball, since it is the team's first try to get the required 10 yards, it is called first down and 10 to go (or first-and-10). Succeeding plays are called second down, third down and *fourth down*. However, as soon as a team crosses the necessary line on any of these plays, the count automatically goes back to first-and-10.

If the offensive team tries 4 straight times to gain the necessary yards but fails, it loses possession of the ball to the opposition *"on downs"*. Therefore, a team that uses up its first 3 downs without achieving a new first down typically uses the fourth down play either to: (1) kick a field goal if it is close enough to make it, or (2) punt the ball (explained below) to make sure the opponent gets possession further back towards its own end zone.

The following is an example of the terminology used: if a team gains 4 yards on first-and-10, the next play is second-and-6 (second down, 6 yards to go = 10 minus 4). If the team then gains 5 more yards on the second down play, it will be left with third-and-1 (third down, 1 yard to go = 6 minus 5).

On that same play, if the team had gained 6 or more yards, it would have achieved a new first down, and the next play would have been first-and-10. When a team has a first down within 10 yards of the opponent's goal line, its necessary line becomes the goal line itself, and it must score a touchdown within 4 plays or lose the ball on downs. This is called *first-and-goal*.

Officials on the field keep track of the number of the down and the amount of yards needed for a first down. A set of officials known as the *chain crew* actually measures first down distances to determine whether or not a team has made the necessary yardage. The progress of an offensive team is measured by how far forward the front of the ball (the end closest to the defense's goal line) has been advanced. The chain crew is discussed further in the chapter entitled **THE OFFICIALS**.

LENGTH OF GAME

A *regulation game* is divided into four *quarters* or *periods*, each lasting 15 minutes. A timing device called the *game clock*, which counts down each quarter by seconds, is displayed on a large scoreboard for spectators and both teams to see at all times. When the game clock expires, the quarter is over, although if a play is in progress at the time, it continues until its completion.

The first and second quarters make up the first half, the third and fourth quarters the second half. Between halves, teams leave the field for a 12-minute rest period called *halftime*, after which a *kickoff* (discussed below) restarts the second half. There is also a short 2-minute break after the first and third quarters when teams switch the ends of the field they are defending.

Although the actual clock time takes only 60 minutes to count down, games usually last about 3 hours because the clock stops frequently throughout the game. The different reasons why the clock is stopped are shown later in this chapter in the section **GAME CLOCK STOPPAGES** on p. 27.

THE PLAY CLOCK

To keep the game moving, a *play clock* limits the time teams may take between plays. One play clock is displayed above each *end zone* to be visible to all players and coaches on the field. After each play is completed, the clocks count down 40 seconds (25 seconds in college) during which the offensive team must start the next play by *snapping* the ball. In professional football, a rule requires that it be set to only 25 seconds in situations where the normal flow of the game has already been stopped, such as by an injury, change of possession or time out. If the clock winds down to 0 before the snap (discussed below) the offense is assessed a penalty for a *delay of game*. The play clock runs independent of whether the game clock is running or stopped.

TIES AND OVERTIME IN PROFESSIONAL FOOTBALL

When a regulation game ends with an equal number of points having been scored by each team, the game is a *tie game*. In professional football, teams play an additional 15-minute period, called *sudden-death overtime* since the first team to score is declared the winner and the game ends.

After a 3-minute *intermission*, the overtime period is started with a coin toss to determine who will get possession of the ball first, the same process that starts the game (see section on **COIN TOSS**). If the overtime period ends with neither team scoring, the game ends in a tie during the regular season. However, in *playoff* games where a winner *must* be declared to eliminate one team from competition, successive 15-minute overtime periods are played, with teams switching sides after each, until one team scores.

COLLEGE FOOTBALL OVERTIME

Until 1995, when the four periods of a college football game ended with the teams tied, there was no overtime and the game ended in a tie. However, beginning in 1996, a new, exciting overtime format was adopted. Now, unlimited extra periods are played until one team ends up with more points than the other.

Each extra period consists of one offensive possession for each team that begins on the opponent's 25-yard line. Each team, when it is on offense, keeps the ball until either it scores, fails to make a first down, or loses possession of the ball. Then, the other team takes possession and makes its own attempt to score from the opponent's 25-yard line. After each team has made its attempt, the one with more points wins.

If neither scores in an extra period or they both score the same number of points, another overtime is played. Beginning with the third overtime, any team that scores a touchdown must attempt a 2-point conversion instead of an extra-point kick.

START OF GAME: THE KICKOFF

Each half of a football game starts with a kickoff (See **Figure 5**), a type of *free kick* where the ball is placed on a 1-inch high plastic *tee* (2-inch in college) at the *kicking team*'s 30-yard line (35 in college) and kicked towards the *receiving team*'s end of the field. Players on the receiving team called *kick returners* try to catch the ball and run with it as far as they can against the kicking team so their team will be as far forward as possible when it becomes the offense on the next play. Players on the kicking team run down the field after the kick to try and stop them, a mission called *covering*

Figure 5: A team kicking off.

the kick. Kickoffs are also kicked by a team after it scores a touchdown or field goal.

In the *NFL*, if a kickoff goes out of bounds before it is touched, the receiving team can choose to take the ball either where the ball left the field or 30 yards from the point of the kick. (Exception: an *onside kick*—described in the next paragraph—must be re-kicked from 5 yards further back.) In college, the receiving team has the option of taking possession 30 yards from the point of the kick or forcing the kicking team to kick off again from 5 yards further back.

A kickoff is a loose ball, so the receiving team needs to pick it up before the kicking team does. Sometimes, the kicking team purposely kicks the ball a shorter distance to give it a better chance of regaining possession of the ball before the receiving team can grab it. This is called an onside kick and is discussed in the chapter entitled **FORMATIONS AND PLAYS**.

COIN TOSS: WHICH TEAM GETS THE BALL FIRST

Before a kickoff begins the game or overtime period, a *coin toss* determines which team kicks and which receives. An official standing in the middle of the field asks the *captain* of the visiting team to call heads or tails and then tosses the coin. The winner of the toss gets to make one of the following two choices and the loser is left with the other:

1) Whether to kick or receive the first kickoff; OR
2) Which end of the field to defend.

At the beginning of the second half, the team that lost the coin toss at the beginning of the game gets to make the choice. Usually, the team that wins the toss decides to receive the kickoff so it can try to score first to gain confidence and momentum. In sudden-death overtime, the coin toss can be critical because if a team chooses to receive the kick and scores on its first possession, the game is over without the other team ever getting the ball.

Sometimes, the winner of the toss will instead choose an end of the field when there is a very strong wind or blinding sun that favors one direction. At the end of the first and third quarters, teams switch sides of the field they are defending.

THE HUDDLE: PLANNING A PLAY

Before most plays, each team gathers around in a *huddle*, a circle of players where the next play is planned. (See **Figure 6**) Usually, one player *calls the play*, giving instructions to the other players who lean over to listen. Huddles minimize the crowd noise to help players hear the call and also reduce the chance of eavesdropping by the opposition. Sometimes, teams plan a

Figure 6: A huddle.

play without a huddle to give the defenders less time to prepare, often catching them off-guard. This is called a *no-huddle offense.*

AT THE LINE: SET-UP FOR A PLAY

Before a play can start, players from each team must face each other from opposing sides of the football. There are two imaginary *lines of scrimmage*, one for each team separated by the length of the ball, which neither team can cross prior to the start of a play. Some players position themselves *on the line* (within 1 yard of it), while others play further back in an area called the *backfield*. The region where the ball is located, between the offensive and defensive lines, is called the *neutral zone*. (See **Figure 7**) Generally, the area that includes both lines and the neutral zone is referred to as the line of scrimmage or "the line".

NEUTRAL ZONE

LINES OF SCRIMMAGE

Figure 7: Players lined up for a play.

An offense must place at least 7 players on the line for every play or it is subject to a penalty. All line players must be "set" (not moving at all) for at least one second when a play begins with the snap. The most common stance is the *3-point stance*, where a player leans forward and places one hand on the ground, preparing himself to charge forward at the snap.

THE SNAP: START OF A PLAY

Each play by the offense begins with the snap, where a player on the offense called the *center* (also called the *snapper*), while facing forward, quickly hands the ball between his legs to a player standing behind him. (See **Figure 8**) One player, usually the *quarterback*, shouts coded signals to the snapper in a rhythm called the *snap count* or *cadence* to indicate exactly when he should snap the ball. The entire offensive team knows the signals, allowing it to get a head start on the defense who does not know them. As soon as the ball is snapped, players on both sides spring into action, hoping to get a quick start on the play.

Figure 8: A snap.

TYPES OF OFFENSIVE PLAYS

There are three main types of *offensive plays*: *running plays*, *passing plays* and *kicking plays*. The ball can be passed forward or kicked only from behind the line of scrimmage, so once the offense has crossed over its line with the ball, it is committed to a running play. Any player who runs with the ball is known as the *ball carrier*. Each of the players mentioned in this section is explained further in the chapter entitled **PLAYER POSITIONS**.

<u>Running Play</u>

Also known as a *rushing play*, the quarterback takes the snap and hands or tosses the ball backward to another player, usually the *running back* or *fullback*, who then tries to advance with it as far as possible. A ball handed to the runner is called a *hand-off* (see **Figure 9**), whereas a ball tossed backward or parallel to the line of scrimmage is called a *pitch-out* or *lateral*. Players on a team can lateral the ball to one another as many times as they want during a play.

<u>Passing Play</u>

The quarterback takes the snap, moves backward a few steps (or "*drops back*") into an imaginary area known as the *pocket* and throws (or "*passes*") the ball forward to a teammate called the *receiver* who tries to catch it and advance. As long as a

Figure 9: A hand-off.

team plans on trying a forward pass, the play is considered a passing play, even if the ball is not thrown and the quarterback ends up running with it. Three things can happen when a forward pass is thrown:

Complete Pass — A receiver catches the ball before it touches the ground and may advance with it until he is tackled or goes out of bounds.

Incomplete Pass — The ball touches the ground before being caught or a receiver catches the ball while out of bounds. The play is over and the ball is returned for the next play to the location where this play began.

Interception — A pass is caught in the air by a defender, creating an instant change of possession. The interceptor can advance it against the passing team until either he is tackled, forced out of bounds or scores.

There are also 3 restrictions on a forward pass:
- Only one forward pass is allowed per play.
- No forward pass may be thrown after a ball carrier has crossed the line of scrimmage.
- A forward pass can be caught only by an *eligible receiver*.

All offensive players are eligible except interior *linemen* (center, *guards* and *tackles*) and (in the NFL) the quarterback. (See **PLAYER POSITIONS**)

Kicking Plays

There are two main types of kicking plays: field goal attempts (also called *place kicks*) and punts.

Field Goal Attempt / Place Kick — A player called the *holder* kneels about 7 yards behind the center, catches a long snap and holds it upright between his fingers and the ground so a *place kicker* can attempt a field goal — a place kick through the goalpost to score points. (See **Figure 10**) No tee is used to elevate the ball off the ground.

Punt — A player called the *punter* standing about 10 yards behind the center catches a long snap sent back to him and kicks the ball into the air towards the other team's end of the field. (See **Figure 11**) The ball must be punted from behind the line of scrimmage. A kick returner on the opposition (called the receiving team) tries to catch the ball and *return* it the other way. He has the following three choices:

- Field the Punt: He can catch the ball and try to run with it if he believes he can gain some yards.

Figure 10: Place kick.

- *Fair Catch*: He can signal for a fair catch by waving one hand, meaning that he will only catch the ball but not advance it. (See **Figure 12**) Although he sacrifices any advance, players on the kicking team are then forbidden from touching him or else they are penalized with a *personal foul*. This minimizes the chance of the returner getting injured or fumbling the ball after a hard tackle.

Figure 11: A punt.

Figure 12: Player signaling a fair catch.

- Let the Ball Go: He can choose not to touch the ball at all. If a punt goes out of bounds, the receiving team takes over where the ball crossed the *sideline*. If it goes into the end zone, it is a *touchback* (explained on p. 24) and the receiving team gets the ball on its own 20-yard line.

Unlike a kickoff which is a loose ball, possession on a punt changes from kicking to receiving team as soon as the ball is kicked. Therefore, players on the receiving team can decide to let the punt go without catching it and their team will still be on offense for the next play. Players on the kicking team who reach the ball first can end the play there by touching or "downing" the ball but do not get possession. Once the ball touches any player on the receiving team, however, it becomes a loose ball and can be *recovered* by either team.

23

Punts are most often kicked by an offense on fourth down when it does not want to take the chance of losing the ball on downs. Instead, it uses that last play to push the opponent back into poorer field position before giving it the ball. Defensive players often try to block punts and field goals by *penetrating* the *offensive line* and raising their arms high into the air.

TOUCHBACK

When a player gets possession of a ball in his own end zone by means of a punt, kickoff, fumble or interception, he has the following option: he can either try to run with the ball out of the end zone, or he can *down* the ball in his end zone by kneeling to the ground on one knee and be awarded a touchback. In a touchback, his team maintains possession of the ball, starts on offense with a first down play on its own 20-yard line, and no points are awarded to either team. A player usually chooses the touchback if he believes that he will not be able to reach the 20-yard line by running out of the end zone with the ball.

STOPPAGES: HOW A PLAY ENDS

Once a play has started with a snap, the ball is said to be *live*, and the play continues until one of several things happens to stop it. In each of the following stoppages, an official blows his whistle to signal the end of the play, the ball is *dead* and the *forward progress* made by the offense is marked by an official who places (*"spots"*) the ball on the ground for the start of the next play:

Tackle — The player with the ball, as a result of contact from a defensive player, touches the ground with any part of his body except his hands or feet, and is considered *down*. In professional football, a player who merely slips and falls down on his own may get up and continue running as long as he is not touched by a defender while still on the ground. In college, however, a player that touches the ground is down whether or not contact by an opponent caused it. At both levels, the ball is spotted where the player was holding it when he first touched the ground.

Forward Progress Stopped — A ball carrier is prevented by defensive players from advancing further, even though he is not tackled. The ball is spotted where the player was holding it when his forward progress was stopped.

Out of Bounds — A ball carrier touches a sideline with any part of his body, or a loose ball touches the ground out of bounds. The ball is spotted where the player first touched out, or in the case of a loose ball, where the ball first touched out of bounds.

Incomplete Pass — A forward pass touches the ground before being caught by any player. The spot of the ball reverts to the previous play's line of scrimmage.

Foul — Certain rule infractions committed by players, called fouls, automatically stop play. These are discussed in detail in the chapter entitled **FOULS AND PENALTIES**.

Scoring — A team scores a touchdown, field goal or safety. The team that scores restarts the game with a kickoff.

Missed Field Goal Attempt — A field goal is wide of the *uprights* or short of the *crossbar*. The play is over and the defense regains possession of the ball at the spot of the kick (or at the previous line of scrimmage in college).

CHANGE OF POSSESSION
When Team A has possession of the ball, Team B can only get it back from a turnover, a punt or on downs.

Turnovers
A turnover is whenever Team A involuntarily loses possession of the ball during a play. The two types are:

Interception — When a defensive player catches a pass thrown forward by an offensive player, it is an interception, and the defender may advance the ball against the offense until either he is tackled, goes out of bounds or scores.

Fumble — Any time a player has possession of a ball and lets go of it before he is down, it is a fumble and the player that regains possession of the ball is said to make the recovery. A backward pass that hits the ground is also considered a fumble. If the ball is jarred loose from a player when he hits the ground, there is no fumble and the ball is dead because the ground cannot cause a fumble. A fumble is only considered a turnover if an opposing player recovers the ball; otherwise, possession still belongs to the same team.

To prevent a team from purposely fumbling the ball forward to gain important yardage, a rule was created that prohibits a team from advancing its own fumble on fourth down or in the last 2 minutes of a half. In an infamous 1978 game, the NFL's Oakland Raiders prompted the creation of this rule with a play known as the *"Holy Roller."* With time running out and his team losing, Raider quarterback Ken Stabler was about to be tackled on the last play of the game when he fumbled the ball forward. His teammates kept the ball rolling forward until it reached the end zone, where Raider Dave Casper fell on it for a game-winning touchdown. If the rule had been in place in 1978, the ball would have been brought back to where Stabler first lost it, and since time had run out, the Raiders would have lost the game.

A ball fumbled out of bounds belongs to the team that last possessed it. If a player fumbles the ball out of bounds in the opponent's end zone, the opponent gets possession on its own 20 yard line. If a player fumbles the ball out of bounds from his own end zone, a safety is awarded to the opponent.

<u>Punt</u>
Team A voluntarily gives the ball to Team B by punting it instead of trying to achieve a first down.

<u>On Downs</u>
When Team A does not make it past the necessary line on a fourth down play, Team B gets possession of the ball where the play ended. If the play was an incomplete pass, Team B gets the ball at the play's line of scrimmage.

GAME CLOCK STOPPAGES

The game clock stops counting down for a number of reasons during the game. These stoppages occur when:

- A team calls *time out*
- Either team scores
- The ball or a player touching the ball is out of bounds
- An incomplete pass is thrown
- The ball changes possession (clock stops after play ends)
- An official calls a foul (clock stops after play ends)
- Officials call time out for an injury
- Officials call time out to discuss a ruling
- Officials call time out to break for TV commercials
- A measurement is taken to tell if a first down was made
- **NFL only**: A player is *sacked* behind the line of scrimmage, except in the last 2 minutes of either half
- **NFL only**: The *2-minute warning* (only 2 minutes remain in a half); if play in progress, clock stops after play ends
- **NFL only**: The *replay assistant* requests a *Referee Replay Review* of a close play after the 2-minute warning of either half or in overtime
- **College only**: The offensive team achieves a first down

TEAM TIME OUTS

Each team is allowed to "call" a maximum of 3 time outs in each half of the game. Time outs stop the game clock when the ball is already dead and allow both teams time to rest and go to the sidelines for coaching advice. Each NFL time out lasts 1 minute and 50 seconds, except during the last 2 minutes of each half when it lasts only 30 seconds. College time outs last 1 minute and 30 seconds unless the requesting team asks for a 30-second time out. The rules prohibit the same team from calling consecutive time outs without a play being run in between. Extra time outs not used in the first half are not carried over into the second half.

In overtime games played during the NFL season, each team gets 2 time outs to use in the overtime period. In college football, each team is allowed one time out in each overtime period. Time outs cannot be carried over from regulation or from one overtime period to another.

INSTANT REPLAY

In 1999 the NFL established a new procedure that gives officials a way to correct certain errors they make on the field. On close plays, a Referee Replay Review can be initiated where the referee runs over to a TV monitor on the sideline and has up to 90 seconds to decide whether there is "indisputable visual evidence" that warrants the reversal of a call on the field. Without such evidence, the original decision must be upheld. A Replay Review can be initiated 2 ways:

1) *Coaches' Challenge*: each team gets only 2 chances per game to dispute a call and must initiate the challenge by calling time out. If the call is reversed, the time out is restored but not the challenge.

2) After the 2-minute warning of either half or in overtime, a *replay assistant* in a broadcast booth can request that any number of close plays be reviewed. No time outs are charged to either team.

The only types of plays that can be reviewed are those where a replay could provide clear evidence to either reverse or uphold a call. These include determining whether a player broke the plane of the goal line for a touchdown, whether he was *in bounds* or out of bounds, whether a pass hit the gound before being caught, and whether a player is officially "down" after contact by a defender.

SUBSTITUTIONS

Substitutes may enter and leave the field freely as long as the ball is dead and one teammate leaves the field for every entering substitute. A team is subject to a penalty if it has more than 11 players on the field when the ball is snapped for the next play, but a team on offense is prohibited from purposely rushing the snap to catch the defense with too many players on the field. In the NFL no penalty is called and the down is replayed. The one exception is: in the last 2 minutes of either half, since time is at a premium, an NFL team may snap the ball as quickly as it wants and catch the opponent with too many men on the field. In college, a penalty of 5 yards is assessed for intentionally rushing the snap at any stage of the game.

SCORING

There are 5 different ways of scoring points in football: a *touchdown, point-after-touchdown (extra point), 2-point conversion, field goal* or *safety*. A team is automatically awarded a fixed number of points for each, as follows:

Touchdown (**6 points**) — The highest-scoring play in football occurs when a team *possesses* a *live ball* in its opponent's *end zone*. This is the ultimate achievement of any offensive *drive*. A touchdown can be scored in one of 3 ways:

• Player carries the ball across opponent's *goal line*
• *Receiver* catches *pass* in opponent's end zone
• Player *recovers loose ball* in opponent's end zone

In the first case where a player is just entering the end zone, it is a touchdown as soon as any part of the ball crosses over any part of an imaginary wall (called a plane) extending straight up from the goal line. (See **Figure 13**) Immediately following a touchdown, the team that scored is given the opportunity to earn extra points.

Figure 13: Touchdown when ball breaks plane of goal line.

Extra Points

On the play after it scores a touchdown, a team has the option of trying either a 2-point conversion or a point-after-touchdown. After one of these attempts, the team that scored the touchdown kicks off to the opposition. An extra point attempt is allowed even if the game clock ran out as the touchdown was scored. It is not allowed after a touchdown in *sudden-death overtime* since the game is over as soon as the touchdown is scored.

Point-After-Touchdown (*PAT*) (**1 point**) — More commonly called the extra point, this is a *place kick* snapped from the 2-yard line (3-yard line in college). The average NFL team succeeds on over 95% of its PAT attempts, so touchdowns are usually worth a total of 7 points (6 for the touchdown + 1 for PAT). If the attempt is "no good", the ball is *dead* and the play is over.

2-point Conversion (**2 points**) — After scoring a touchdown, a team runs a single play from the 2-yard line (3-yard line in college), and if it scores what would normally be a touchdown, it is awarded 2 points. The 1994 season was the first time that *NFL* rules allowed this 2-point option, the first change in its scoring rules in 75 years, although it has been available in college since 1958. A team behind in the score by 8 points can now tie the game with a touchdown and 2-point conversion, making it easier for losing teams to catch up quickly. However, teams not desperate to score 2 points still rely mostly on the higher-percentage PAT.

Field Goal (**3 points**) — A player snaps the ball backwards about 7 yards to a *holder* who stands it on the ground for a *place kicker* to boot through the *goalpost* in the back of the end zone. The kick must pass above the *crossbar* and between the *uprights* to count (or be "good"). Otherwise, the kick is "no good" and no points are awarded. A ball kicked high above the top of the goalpost is judged on whether it would have passed between the uprights if they extended upward to that height.

The distance of a field goal is measured from the place of the kick to the goalpost. To calculate it, you generally add

17 to the yard line of the *line of scrimmage*. For example, if the line of scrimmage is the 30-yard line, the field goal would be from about 47 yards (30 + 17 = 47). This includes 7 yards from kicker to the line, 30 more to the goal line and 10 more to the goalpost.

After a team kicks a successful field goal, it then kicks off to the opposition. In the NFL, if a team misses a field goal attempt, the defense regains possession of the ball at the spot of the kick instead of where the play started. This gives the ball to the defense about 7 yards closer to the offense's goal line, discouraging the offense from attempting long field goals where the likelihood of missing is greater. (In collegiate play, the defense takes over at the previous line of scrimmage.) If a team misses a field goal between the opponent's goal line and 20-yard line (*inside* the 20), its opponent gets to move the ball out to its 20-yard line to start its next offensive drive.

Safety (**2 points**) — When a ball carrier is tackled in his own end zone after bringing the ball there under his own power, the opposing team earns 2 points. A safety is also called on a team that commits a *foul* while in possession of the ball in its own end zone, or on a team that fumbles the ball out of bounds in its own end zone. A safety is not called when a player is tackled in his own end zone after receiving a kick or intercepting a ball there because the opposing team caused the ball to be there. Similarly, when a player is stopped in front of his own end zone and forced back into it by the defense, a safety is not scored because when his *forward motion* ceased, the play was over before he went into the end zone.

When Team A suffers a safety, not only does Team B get 2 points, but Team A must give the ball back to Team B using a *free kick* from its own 20-yard line, either by punting, *drop kicking* or place kicking it to the opposition.

The next chapter entitled **PLAYER SKILLS** describes the many talents and techniques required to play football.

PLAYER SKILLS

Football players need certain *offensive* and *defensive* skills to compete effectively. *Offensive players* need to be adept at *blocking*, *passing*, *receiving* and running with the football, while *defensive players* have to be skilled at *tackling* and *pass coverage*. *Special teams* players such as *kickers* also must have certain abilities. The various *positions* on a team require a different mix of these skills. Although mentioned here, more detailed descriptions are in the next chapter on **PLAYER POSITIONS.**

OFFENSIVE SKILLS

<u>Blocking</u>

Blocking is the act of preventing a defensive player from getting to the *ball carrier* or runner. Without blocking, 11 defensive players would all chase after the player with the ball, making it nearly impossible for him to advance. To prevent this, most players on offense act as blockers and are responsible for blocking at least one defensive player, leaving the ball carrier far fewer defenders to run past or *beat*. When two blockers are assigned to block one particularly dangerous defender, it is called a *double team*.

Blockers use their arms and bodies to keep defenders away from their teammate who has the ball. (See **Figure 14**) However, a *foul* for *holding* or *facemask* is called against the offense if a blocker uses his hands or arms to grasp or hook a defender, his uniform or his equipment.

Blockers are also not allowed to hit defenders below the waist from behind, called *clipping*. (Except when an *offensive lineman* blocks a *defensive lineman* at the *line of scrimmage*.) Furthermore, an offensive player may not block below the waist a defender who is already being blocked by another offensive player (called a *chop block*). These fouls and their consequences are explained further in the chapter entitled **FOULS & PENALTIES.**

BALL CARRIER   BLOCKER   DEFENDER

Figure 14: Blocking.

There are two fundamentally different types of blocking:

- *Run Blocking*: As soon as the ball is *snapped*, blockers blast forward to push defenders off *the line* to make room for the runner on a *running play*. Often, two or more blockers coordinate their movements to force defenders away from an area the runner will be entering, called *opening a hole*. On some plays, speedier run blockers on a team, such as the *tight end* or *fullback*, try to push across the line of scrimmage themselves to clear a path for the ball carrier running behind them, called a *lead block*. On other plays, offensive linemen *pull* or leave their position to run parallel to the line of scrimmage, providing a lead block for the runner.

- *Pass Blocking*: After the snap on a *passing play*, blockers stay at the line or retreat a little, absorbing the impact of any defensive players who *rush* or charge towards the *quarterback*. The goal of the blockers is to keep the defenders away from the passer for as long as possible, giving him more time to find an *open* receiver (one who is not guarded closely) and pass him the ball.

Running with the Ball

Several skills help a ball carrier to avoid defenders and advance the ball *down the field* (towards the opponent's goal). First, a runner should try to follow his blockers, running in areas already cleared of defenders. Second, good runners often make sudden changes in direction, called *cut backs*, which force defenders also to change direction and lose their momentum. (See **Figure 15**) Third, a runner can try to ward off those tacklers that reach him by pushing them away with his free arm (the one not holding the ball), called a *stiff arm* or *straight arm*. Finally, a runner must protect the ball from being knocked away or stolen by defenders to prevent a *fumble* and a possible loss of *possession*.

Figure 15: **Runner performing a cut back.**

Passing

Passes are typically thrown by a team's quarterback to a receiver running down the field. Because of the football's odd shape, it must be thrown with a spin (called a *spiral*) to get distance and accuracy. (See **Figure 16**) In a well-thrown spiral, the ball points in the same direction during its entire flight, giving it less wind resistance and making it easier to catch than a pass that tumbles or wobbles. A particularly good spiral that does not wobble at all is called a "tight spiral".

Figure 16: A spiral vs. non-spiral pass.

The most important part of passing is ball placement, as inaccurate passes fall to the ground *incomplete* or may be *intercepted* by the defense. A passer must throw the ball ahead of the receiver to a spot where the receiver will be running to, called *leading the receiver*. A pass aimed directly at a moving receiver will be too far behind him by the time it reaches him. Finally, the ball should be thrown only to receivers who are open enough to catch it. Even accurate passes may be intercepted if a receiver is surrounded by 2 or 3 defenders (called *double* or *triple coverage*).

Receiving
Receiving is the act of catching passes thrown by a teammate, usually the quarterback, and it requires several key skills. Foremost, receivers need to find a way to get open — to create space between them and their defenders — to allow them a clear shot at catching the ball. On most plays, receivers follow paths called *pass patterns* or *routes* that are pre-determined by a play called in the *huddle*. Routes that are run accurately help the passer quickly locate a receiver so he can throw to the right spot.

The other major skill required of receivers is catching the football. Receivers must have good hands and great concentration to catch the ball and hold onto it with defenders ready to crush them. In addition, if a receiver catches the ball at a *sideline*, he needs to touch the ground with either both of his feet or any other part of his body completely *in bounds* or else the pass is incomplete. However, if a receiver was pushed out of bounds by a defender after catching a pass, but would otherwise have been in bounds, the pass is considered complete. In college, a receiver needs to touch only one foot in bounds for the pass to be *complete*, but there is no provision to award him a complete pass if he is forced out by a defender. (See **Figure 17**)

Figure 17: A receiver in bounds (solid line) and out of bounds (dotted line). Both are considered in bounds in college.

DEFENSIVE SKILLS

Tackling

Tackling is the essence of defense — stopping the ball carrier by forcing him to the ground. Good tacklers usually try to wrap their arms around the ball carrier's legs, making it impossible for him to run any further. (See **Figure 18**) A defender who tries to tackle a player's upper body may be thrown completely aside by a stiff arm or might be dragged for many yards as a runner's powerful

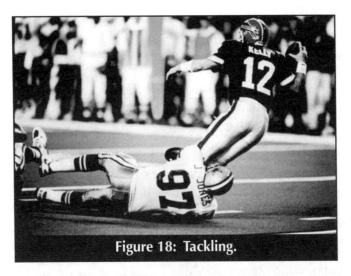

Figure 18: Tackling.

legs carry both of them forward. No defender may tackle a player who does not have the ball (a holding foul) or grab a player's facemask when tackling him (a facemask foul).

Pass Coverage

Certain defenders are assigned to pass coverage — the task of running with receivers and preventing them from catching passes. Pass coverage is a difficult job because a defender must stay close to a receiver without knowing ahead of time which way he is going. Complicating the defender's job is that he must pursue just the ball, contacting the receiver no earlier than the moment the ball arrives, or he is guilty of *pass interference*. However, the defender is permitted to come into contact with a pass receiver once at the beginning of a play, as long as it is no more than 5 yards beyond the line of scrimmage (1 yard in college). To take advantage of this, most pass defenders use the *bump-and-run* technique, where they hit a receiver once when he is coming off the line of scrimmage to slow him down before following him to prevent him from catching a pass.

A good pass defender must anticipate where the ball will be thrown and move quickly to deflect it with his hand, intercept it or, as a last resort, tackle the receiver after he has made the catch. Timing, concentration, speed and leaping ability are essential skills for this task.

KICKING SKILLS
Punting

Punters have three objectives for their kicks: distance, height and accuracy. A long distance kick is necessary because the *punt returner* is forced to start his *runback* from deeper (further back) in his own *territory*. However, a high kick is also important to give the *kicking team* enough time to run down the field and tackle the returner or force him to call for a *fair catch*. The time that a punted ball is in the air is called its *hang time*. The longer the hang time, the better the punt.

Accuracy is critical for a punter when kicking in his opponent's half of the field. Since a long kick would go into the opponent's *end zone* for a *touchback* (automatically allowing the receiving team to start *on offense* at its own 20-yard line), a punter kicks the ball towards the corner of the field to try to place it *out of bounds* just before it reaches the *goal line*. If he succeeds, the receiving team goes on offense where the ball crossed the sideline, deep in its own territory

The next chapter on **PLAYER POSITIONS** describes which skills are most important for different players to have.

PLAYER POSITIONS

Football players must carry out a wide variety of tasks over the course of a game, so each team assigns individuals to specialized *positions* where their physical abilities are best matched with their roles. (See **Figure 19**) When organized football was first played, the same participants played at both offensive and defensive positions. Today, most players occupy a position on either the *offensive* or *defensive unit*, but not both. Other players known as *special teams players* participate only on *kicking plays* (*kickoffs*, *punts* and *place kicks*).

A player on the offensive unit waits on the *sidelines* while his team's defensive unit tries to stop the opposition. As soon as his team regains *possession* of the ball, the entire offensive unit replaces the entire defensive unit on the field, which is why you see so many players running on and off the field every time the ball changes hands. Football is unique in this way — in no other team sport do completely separate groups of players split the tasks of offense and defense.

Before the start of every play, 11 offensive and defensive players from opposite teams line up on opposite sides of the *line of scrimmage* in an arrangement called a *formation*. Each team chooses a formation that allows it to best carry out a particular type of offensive or defensive strategy. All formations place some players at the line of scrimmage and other players behind them (in the *backfield*). An offense is required to place at least 7 players *on the line* for every play; there is no such requirement for the defense. The different formations and their use are discussed further in the chapter entitled **FORMATIONS AND PLAYS**.

Each *NFL* team is allowed to carry a *roster* of 53 players who are eligible to play in a game, of which only 11 may be on the *field* at one time. Therefore, each player who plays at the start of a game (called a *starter*) has at least one *backup* who can replace him on the field when he becomes tired or if he sustains an injury. The coach names up to 6 team *captains* before each game. One captain on the offensive unit and another on the defensive unit are responsible both for calling the *coin toss* and for responding to *fouls* called by the *officials* (by either *accepting* or *declining* the *penalties*).

The following is a description of each player position (the abbreviations in parentheses are used in printed team rosters):

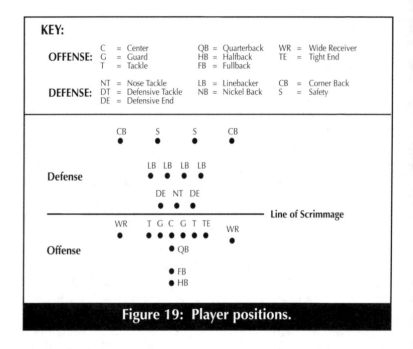

Figure 19: Player positions.

THE OFFENSIVE UNIT

Quarterback (QB) — Today's stars: *Kurt Warner, Brett Favre,* Rich Gannon, Jeff Garcia — He is the centerpiece of a team's offense, making the critical decisions on how to distribute the ball to his teammates. After taking the *snap* from the center, he either hands the ball to a *running back* to run with, *passes* it to a *receiver* or runs with it himself. Before each play, the quarterback *huddles* with the other offensive players to communicate which play they will attempt. These plays are either signaled to him by a coach on the sidelines or called by the quarterback himself. Since 1994, a *radio* has been allowed in the NFL to transmit the plays from the coach to the quarterback through a tiny receiver in his helmet until 15 seconds remain on the *play clock*.

Once the teams line up for a play, the quarterback is responsible for *reading the defense* (recognizing their formation) prior to the snap and yelling a set of verbal commands called an *audible* to change the play if necessary. Then, the quarterback shouts the *cadence* or *snap count* to indicate when he wants the center to snap him the ball.

Several traits make for a good quarterback. Foremost, he should have good visual recognition to quickly locate *"open" receivers*, a strong throwing arm to *lead* them with accurate *spirals* from a distance and a quick release to get rid of the ball before he is *sacked* (*tackled* behind the line of scrimmage for a loss). He also needs to be mentally sharp to communicate the plays to his teammates and make split-second decisions on how to get them the ball. Tall quarterbacks have an advantage (most in the NFL are at least 6-foot-2) because they can see their receivers above huge *linemen* and throw them the ball without having the linemen knock it down. Finally, it helps for a quarterback to be quick and agile to elude a defensive *pass rush* and avoid being sacked (called *scrambling*).

Because of the importance of the quarterback in football, rules have been enacted to help protect him from injury, including *roughing the passer* which prohibits defenders from intentionally trying to harm him. (See the chapter entitled **FOULS AND PENALTIES**.) One controversial rule used to encourage officials to blow the whistle and stop play as soon as a quarterback was *"in the grasp* and control" of a defender, even before he was tackled. The rule was broadly criticized for denying the quarterback a chance of escaping the clutches of a tackler. In recent years, it has only been enforced when the safety of the quarterback is clearly in jeopardy.

Running Backs — Today's stars: *Marshall Faulk*, Edgerrin James, Eddie George, Curtis Martin — At the beginning of most plays, there are one or two offensive players positioned behind the quarterback known as the running backs or just the *backs*. There are two different types of running backs — the *halfback* and the *fullback*, although some teams do not distinguish between the two, labeling them both as running backs and having them share the duties of both positions.

Halfback (HB) — This versatile player carries the ball on the majority of his team's *running plays* and receives many short forward passes. He also helps *block* for the quarterback on passing plays and for the fullback on running plays, even throwing a pass himself on rare occasions. Good halfbacks have a combination of quick acceleration to squeeze through *holes* opened by the *offensive linemen*, sharp *cut backs* to elude tacklers, and good receiving skills to catch passes when the quarterback is being rushed and the other receivers are *covered*.

Fullback (FB) — His primary role is to block for the halfback and provide the quarterback with *pass protection*, but he also runs with the ball in *short yardage* situations (when only a few yards are needed, like *first-and-goal)* and catches short forward passes. As a result, he is generally a larger, more powerful player than the halfback — a slower runner but a better *blocker*.

Wide Receiver (WR) — Today's stars: *Randy Moss*, Marvin Harrison, Terrell Owens, *Jerry Rice* — His role is to catch the majority of his team's forward passes, especially the longer ones. Before the snap, 1, 2 or 3 wide receivers position themselves wide to the left or right of the offensive line where they have open space to start running their *pass patterns*. Wide receivers need to be able to run fast and change directions quickly to get "open" from speedy defenders guarding them and avoid being tackled after a catch. They must also have good hands to catch passes that arrive high and low from a variety of angles and be willing to dive through the air to snare passes in acrobatic fashion.

Tight End (TE) — Today's stars: Tony Gonzalez, Shannon Sharpe, Frank Wycheck — A hybrid of the wide receiver and the offensive lineman (discussed below), the tight end both catches passes and blocks. He lines up between the wide receivers and the offensive linemen, tight to the end of the line (thus his title). Whichever side he plays on is called the *strong side* because of the extra blocking he provides (the opposite side is called the *weak side*). Tight ends are much larger (usually weighing over 230 pounds) and stronger than wide receivers so they can block large defenders, but they must also be good receivers.

Offensive Linemen (OL): *Center* (C), *Guards* (G) and *Tackles* (OT) — Today's stars: Larry Allen, Jonathen Ogden — These players are positioned at the line of scrimmage to block defensive players, opening holes on running plays and providing pass protection on *passing plays*. It is their responsibility to provide the quarterback with enough time to find a receiver and pass him the ball. The offensive linemen are the only offensive players besides the quarterback who are *ineligible* to catch forward passes (in college, even the quarterback is eligible). To become eligible, they must notify the referee and stand at least one yard behind the line of scrimmage prior to the snap.

Offensive linemen are among the largest (often weighing over 300 pounds) and strongest members of any football team since they must be able to fight off the biggest and meanest defensive players. They must also have quick feet and good blocking technique to stay in front of these defenders. The 3 types of offensive linemen have these different functions:

- Center: He stands in the middle of the line and snaps the ball to begin every play
- Guards: The left and right guards play furthest inside on the line, to each side of the center
- Tackles: The left and right tackles play outside of the guards

THE DEFENSIVE UNIT
Defensive Linemen (DL): *Tackles* (DT) and *Ends* (DE) — Today's stars: Michael Strahan, Warren Sapp — These players are a team's first line of defense, fighting off the blocking of offensive linemen to try and tackle the *ball carrier*. On running plays, they try to stop the runner before he advances too far past the line of scrimmage, and on passing plays, they try to break through the line to rush the quarterback and sack him. One or two defensive tackles play in the center of

the defensive line and two defensive ends play on the outside. In defensive formations using only a single tackle, that player is called the *nose tackle*.

Defensive linemen are the largest and strongest defensive players, and they must be aggressive enough to fight through the blocks of huge offensive linemen. They must also be fast enough to chase after and tackle running backs and quarterbacks carrying the ball.

Linebackers (LB) — Today's stars: Ray Lewis, Junior Seau, Derrick Brooks — Positioned behind the defensive linemen, these players are a team's second line of defense, tackling runners who get past the linemen and dropping back to cover receivers on passing plays. A team usually plays with 3 or 4 linebackers depending on the formation. Linebackers are the most versatile defensive players, strong and aggressive enough to fight off larger and more powerful blockers, yet fast enough to follow receivers and prevent them from catching passes.

Defensive Backs (DB): *Safeties* (S) and *Cornerbacks* (CB) — Today's stars: John Lynch, Aeneas Williams, Darren Sharper — These players are positioned to the rear of a defensive unit in the backfield and act as the last line of defense. Their main job is covering the wide receivers on passing plays to knock the ball away and make *interceptions*. They also perform the critical task of pursuing runners who have made it past the rest of the defense, stopping them with one-on-one tackles, also called *open-field tackles*. The safeties play towards the center of the field, and the cornerbacks more towards the outside, closer to the sidelines.

Defensive backs must be very fast and agile to keep up with the great speed of the receivers and have good jumping ability to reach passes thrown high into the air.

SPECIAL TEAMS

A special-teams player is any player who participates in a kicking play. On kickoffs and punts, this includes every player on the *kicking team* who tries to tackle the *kick returner* (called *kickoff* or *punt coverage*) and every player on the *receiving team* who tries to block for the returner. With both sides running at full speed towards each other, the potential for injury is high. Coaches often put their youngest and most aggressive players on special teams because they are not afraid to play with reckless abandon. The following are some key special teams players:

Place Kicker (PK) — Today's stars: Matt Stover, Jason Elam — He kicks off and attempts all of a team's field goals and *points-after-touchdown*, so he must have a strong and accurate kicking leg. In the past decade, place kickers who kick the ball with the instep of the foot have become prevalent. They are known as *soccer*-style kickers because they approach the ball from the side and kick it like soccer players kick a soccer ball.

Punter (P) — Today's stars: Shane Lechler, Darren Bennett — His role is to punt the ball. He must have good hands to catch the long snap from the center, a strong leg to kick the ball far and high (good *hang time*), and accuracy to kick the ball *out of bounds* just in front of the opposition's goal line.

Holder (H) — He catches the ball snapped from the center, places it on the ground vertically and holds it there for the place kicker to attempt a field goal or extra point. The position is often played by one of a team's *backup* quarterbacks who has much experience from receiving snaps in practice.

Kick Returner (KR) — Today's stars: Jermaine Lewis, Darrick Vaughn — On a punt or kickoff, he stands at the rear of a receiving team and tries to catch the kicked ball and return it as far as possible. Kick returners are usually very fast and light so they can outrun the kick coverage in the open field to make long *runbacks*.

The next section on the **OFFICIALS** describes the people who maintain the order in this fast and rough sport.

THE OFFICIALS

The conduct of an *NFL* football game is controlled by a *crew of 7 officials* — the *referee, umpire, head linesman, line judge, side judge, back judge* and *field judge* — who work together to make sure the game is played according to the rules. College rules allow between 4 and 7 officials — the first 4 listed above are required. Each official stands in a specific area on the *field* for each play as shown in **Figure 20**. While an official is allowed to call any penalty he observes, his position on the field usually limits what he is capable of seeing to his immediate area. A 3-man *chain crew* assists the officials by measuring the *offensive team*'s progress, and a *replay assistant* determines which plays deserve a *Referee Replay Review* after the *2-minute warning* of either half or in *overtime*.

The officials wear special uniforms that include a black and white striped shirt, white pants, striped socks and a cap with a visor. The referee wears a white cap while the other officials wear a black cap. Each official carries with him a *whistle* that he blows to signal that the ball is *dead*, and a weighted bright gold *penalty flag* to signal that a *foul* is being called.

When an official observes a player or his team violating a rule, he signals a *foul* by tossing his flag. The officials then hold a brief conference on the field to sort out what each saw and assess the proper *penalty*. Once they have decided, the referee uses a small wireless microphone to announce over the stadium loudspeaker the type of foul, the uniform number of the offending player, and which team he plays for. At the same time, he uses a set of gestures to signal the foul so that coaches and spectators who could not hear the announcement still understand what the call is. (See **OFFICIALS' HAND SIGNALS** at the end of this book.)

THE REFEREE
The referee is the chief official, responsible for overseeing the general conduct and control of the game. He is the final authority in any disputes that arise regarding *scoring, downs* or any other matter not specifically assigned to another

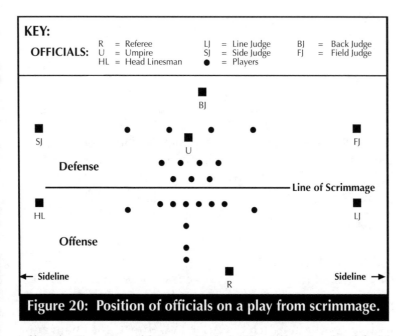

Figure 20: Position of officials on a play from scrimmage.

official. Because of his position in the offensive backfield, he watches for possible *holding* fouls by *offensive linemen* and *illegal motion* by any of the *backs*.

When any official calls a foul, the referee gives the appropriate hand signal, provides each team's *captain* with the details of the foul and presents the captain of the non-offending team with the option of *accepting* or *declining* the penalty (discussed in the chapter on **FOULS AND PENALTIES**). Among the referee's other duties are placing the ball at the correct spot for the start of each play, signaling to the *play clock* operator when to restart his clock after a play *stoppage* and reviewing close plays on *instant replay* to determine whether the decision on the field should be changed.

A player who disagrees with the decision of any official may protest only to the referee, and the argument must center on how the official interpreted a rule and not on his judgment. The referee is also the only official who can order the chain crew to make a measurement to see if a team has made a *first down* when the ball is close to the *necessary line*. Even when the referee decides not to order a measurement, coaches often ask him to reconsider when they believe the outcome will help their team.

THE UMPIRE

The umpire stands in the *defensive backfield* and has two important duties. First, he inspects players' equipment before the game to make sure it does not violate the rules. Second, he watches the conduct of players at the *line of scrimmage* to see if an offensive player is guilty of a *false start*, illegal motion or holding, or if any player is *offside*. In addition to his main duties, the umpire also determines whether there are *ineligible linemen downfield* during a *passing play* and keeps the *score* of the game.

THE HEAD LINESMAN

Positioned at the line of scrimmage near one *sideline*, the head linesman is a key member of the officiating crew because he tracks the *forward progress* of the offensive team, marking it with his foot after each play. He also directs the chain crew to reposition the *measuring sticks* whenever a team starts a new *series of downs*. Because of his position on the field, he also watches for fouls at the line of scrimmage, such as offside and illegal motion.

THE LINE JUDGE

Positioned at the line of scrimmage across the field from the head linesman, the line judge oversees the timing of the game. He times the game with a clock he carries in case the *official game clock* fails, times the *intermission* between *halves* and fires a blank pistol to signal the end of each *period*. The line judge also assists the other officials with calling penalties at the line, and on his side of the field he marks the spot where a ball goes *out of bounds*.

THE SIDE JUDGE

The side judge stands behind the defense on the same side of the field as the head linesman. From there, he observes the conduct of players once they have moved into his side of the defensive backfield, too far away for the head linesman or umpire to see. He determines where a ball that went out of bounds crosses the sideline, and he carefully watches passing plays to judge if a pass is *complete* and whether any player commits *pass interference*.

THE FIELD JUDGE

The field judge stands behind the defense on the same side as the line judge, performing the same duties as the side judge but on the opposite side of the field. In addition, on *field goal* or *point-after-touchdown* attempts, the field judge stands on the *end line* underneath one of the *uprights* of the *goalpost* (the back judge stands under the other) to judge if the *kick* is *good*.

THE BACK JUDGE

The back judge is positioned furthest back in the defensive backfield of any official, and his main duty is to observe conduct in that area on *punts*, *kickoffs* and passes thrown into the defensive *end zone*, especially when these plays are out of the other officials' sight range. He is also in charge of timing the interval between plays using the *play clock*, the length of all team time outs and the intermission between the two periods of each half. Finally, on field goal and extra point attempts, he stands under one upright of the goalpost (the field judge stands under the other) to observe if the kick is good.

OTHER OFFICIALS
Chain Crew

These 3 assistants to the main officials, called crewmen, count the downs and track the yardage required for a first down. One crewman holds a *down marker* which displays the number of the down a team is playing. The other two crewmen called *rodmen* hold measuring sticks on the sidelines that are connected by a *chain* exactly 10 yards apart. (See **Figure 21**) One stick marks the position of the ball when a team begins a new set of downs, and the second marks the team's necessary line, 10 yards away.

When the referee asks for a measurement to determine if a team has made a first down, the two rodmen run out onto the field carrying the measuring sticks to see if the front of the ball has made it past the front stick. The necessary line and the position of the sticks only change when a team advances past this front marker to earn a new first down (called *moving the chains*) or when it loses *possession* of the ball. **49**

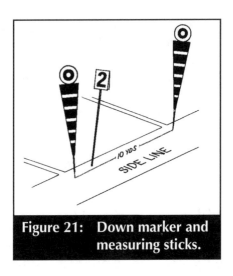

Figure 21: Down marker and measuring sticks.

Official Scorers

These officials are not part of the field crew, but they record numerous individual and team statistics, such as how and when points are scored, and how many yards are gained. Most of the statistics they record are described in the chapter entitled **DECIPHERING FOOTBALL STATISTICS**.

Replay Assistant

When the NFL established a new *instant replay* prodedure in 1999, it added this official to sit in the broadcast booth to determine which close plays deserve a Referee Replay Review after the 2-minute warning of either half or in overtime. During these times, the replay assistant signals to the referee that a play should be reviewed, but during the rest of the game, only a *Coaches' Challenge* can initiate a review. (See page 28 for a full explanation of the instant replay rule). On all reviewed plays, the referee watches the replay on a field-level TV monitor and has up to 90 seconds to determine whether "indisputable visual evidence" exists to reverse the call made on the field. Otherwise, the original call is upheld.

Now that we have met the officials, it is time to discuss their main job — calling **FOULS AND PENALTIES**.

FOULS AND PENALTIES

When an *official* catches any player breaking one of football's many rules, he calls a *foul* and punishes the player with a *penalty*. Fouls can be committed by an offensive player, a defensive player or either team. The purpose of a penalty is to move the team that broke the rule further away from its objective — the opponent's *goal line*. The distance that a team is moved is usually between 5 and 15 yards, depending on the severity of the foul.

When an official sees a violation, he throws his bright gold *penalty flag*. Depending on the type of foul, he either blows his whistle to stop the play immediately or lets the play run its natural course. Then, the referee asks the captain of the non-guilty team whether he would like to *accept* or *decline* the penalty against his opponent, and the referee places the ball at the appropriate spot for the next play. The referee uses a set of hand signals to tell the players and the crowd which foul he has called. The signals for the most common fouls are illustrated at the end of this book in the chapter entitled **OFFICIALS' HAND SIGNALS**.

Since there are well over 100 different fouls in football, they will not all be mentioned in this book. The most common fouls are listed in **Table 1** and described in this chapter.

ACCEPTING OR DECLINING A PENALTY

When the captain of the non-guilty team is given the option of accepting or declining a penalty, he is really being given the following choice:

- Accepting: Asking the referee to move the guilty team backwards. If a play was in progress when the foul was called, it does not count and the *down* is replayed.

- Declining: Refusing the penalty yards and letting the results of the previous play stand. A down is used up on the play.

TABLE 1: MOST COMMON PENALTIES

Key:

Off / Def: Whether the foul can be an offensive foul, defensive foul or both

Yards: The number of yards the penalized team loses

Previous Spot: The line of scrimmage for the previous play

Succeeding Spot: The line of scrimmage for the next play if there had been no penalty

* Spot varies: Spot depends on other factors, explained in **Table 3**

** Different in college; see detailed description of foul

*** Non-offending team chooses

**** Repeat Down for offensive foul, Automatic 1st Down for defensive foul

(D) Dead Ball Foul

FOUL	OFF/ DEF	YARDS	MEASURED FROM	EFFECT ON DOWN
FOULS AT THE BEGINNING OF A PLAY				
Delay of Game (D)	Offense	5	Line of Scrimmage	Repeat Down
Encroachment (D)	Off or Def	5	Line of Scrimmage	Repeat Down
False Start (D)	Offense	5	Line of Scrimmage	Repeat Down
Illegal Formation	Offense	5	Previous Spot	Repeat Down
Illegal Motion	Offense	5	Previous Spot	Repeat Down
Offside	Off or Def	5	Previous Spot	Repeat Down
Too Many Men on the Field	Off or Def	5	Previous Spot	Repeat Down
FOULS THAT OCCUR DURING PLAY				
Facemask (incidental)	Off or Def	5	Spot varies *	Repeat Down
Holding	Offense	10	Spot varies *	Repeat Down
Holding	Defense	5**	Spot varies *	Automatic 1st Down

52

Foul	Against	Yards	Spot	Loss of Down in NFL only
Illegal Forward Pass (pass thrown from beyond line)	Offense	5	Spot of Pass	Repeat Down
Illegal Forward Pass (2nd pass or pass after ball has crossed line of scrimmage)	Offense	5	Previous Spot	Repeat Down
Illegal Forward Pass (to ineligible receiver)	Offense	5	Previous Spot	Repeat Down
Illegal Use of Hands	Offense	10	Spot varies *	Repeat Down
Illegal Use of Hands	Defense	5**	Previous Spot	Automatic 1st Down
Ineligible Member of Kicking Team Downfield	Offense	5	Previous Spot	Repeat Down
Ineligible Receiver Downfield	Offense	5	Previous Spot	Repeat Down
Intentional Grounding	Offense	0*** or 10***	Spot of Foul	Loss of Down
			Previous Spot	Loss of Down
Pass Interference	Defense	0**	Spot of Foul	Automatic 1st Down
Pass Interference	Offense	10**	Previous Spot	Repeat Down
Running into the Kicker	Defense	5	Previous Spot	Repeat Down
PERSONAL FOULS THAT OCCUR DURING PLAY				
Chop Block (Illegal Cut)	Offense	15	Spot varies *	Repeat Down
Clipping	Off or Def	15	Spot varies *	****
Facemask (flagrant)	Off or Def	15	Spot varies *	****
Illegal Block Below the Waist	Off or Def	15	Spot varies *	****
Roughing the Kicker	Defense	15	Previous Spot	Automatic 1st Down
Roughing the Passer	Defense	15	Previous Spot**	Automatic 1st Down
Unnecessary Roughness	Off or Def	15	Spot varies *	****
FOUL THAT CAN OCCUR ANYTIME				
Unsportsmanlike Conduct	Off or Def	15	Succeeding Spot	****

In most cases, it makes sense for the captain to accept a penalty only if taking the penalty yards will leave his team in a better situation than just keeping the previous play. Therefore, the accept/decline decision often depends on the outcome of the play, as the example in **Table 2** shows.

TABLE 2: EXAMPLE OF ACCEPT/DECLINE DECISION

Situation: Second down, 8 yards to go
Foul: Offside called against the offense during the play
Penalty: 5 yards and replay the down
Situation if penalty is accepted: Second-and-13
The defensive captain's accept/decline decision depends on what happened during the play. Below are some examples:

Results of Play	Captain's Decision
If offense gained 12 yards	The offense only needed 8 yards for a new first down, so gaining 12 would be enough for a new first down. Therefore, the defensive captain will accept the penalty because it wipes out the play and leaves the offense with second-and-13.
If offense lost 7 yards	Since the offense lost more yards on the play (7) then than it would from the penalty (5) the defense will decline the penalty to keep the results of the play.
If offense gained 1 yard	Declining the penalty leaves the offense with a third-and-7, compared to a second-and-13 for accepting. The defense will accept the penalty if it would rather push the offense back 6 more yards (13 to go vs. 7 to go) in exchange for giving it another play (second down vs. third down).

CONSEQUENCES OF A PENALTY

In some situations, even a minor penalty call can have major consequences. For example, if a team scores a touchdown on an 80-yard run but one of its players is called for a *holding* penalty (only a 10-yard penalty), the defense will accept the penalty, wiping out the score and forcing the offense to replay the down from 10 yards further back. This 10-yard penalty actually cost the offense 90 yards and 6 points.

MEASURING PENALTY YARDAGE

If a penalty is accepted, the referee picks up the ball, walks with it the penalized number of yards towards the guilty team's goal line, and puts it back down at a new spot for the start of the next play. Penalty yardage is measured from one of 3 locations, depending on the type of foul and when it occurred:

- *Previous spot*: where the ball was snapped from to start the last play
- *Succeeding spot*: where the ball would be put in play next if there was no penalty
- *Spot of foul*: where the foul was committed

Any foul that occurs between plays is called a *dead ball foul*, and the penalty is always assessed from the succeeding spot. The correct spot for any other foul is listed later in this chapter next to the description of each foul, and also in **Table 1**. For some fouls, you will also need to consult **Table 3** to determine what the correct spot should be.

TABLE 3: OTHER PENALTY ENFORCEMENT SPOTS		
Type of Play	**Condition**	**Spot**
Passing Play	Personal foul-- defense prior to completed pass	Previous Spot or Succeeding Spot, chosen by offense
	All other fouls	Previous Spot
Running Play	Offensive foul	Spot of Foul or Succeeding Spot, whichever is worse for the offense, but no worse than Previous Spot
	Defensive foul	If play gained yards: • Succeeding Spot If play lost yards: • Previous Spot for fouls beyond line of scrimmage • Succeeding Spot or Spot of Foul for fouls behind the line, whichever is best for the offense
Kicking Play	Foul by receiving team after kick	Spot of Foul, Succeeding Spot, or Spot where possession is gained, whichever is worse for receiving team
	All other fouls	Previous Spot

There are 4 things to keep in mind about measuring penalties:

- If a penalty assessed against the defense moves the ball ahead of the offensive team's *necessary line*, the offense gets a new first down.
- Any penalty that would move a team more than halfway from the measuring spot to the closest goal line is moved only to the halfway point. This rule was established to prevent a penalty from moving a team over the goal line for a score.
- When an offensive team commits a foul in its own *end zone*, the defense is awarded a *safety*.
- When a team scores a *touchdown*, *field goal*, *2-point conversion* or *extra point* despite a defensive foul, the penalty is assessed from the spot of the ensuing kickoff.

FOULS WITH CHANGE OF POSSESSION

If a foul is committed during a play where there is a *change of possession*, exactly when the foul occurred affects which team keeps the ball. Looking at a punt, interception or fumble as an event, if a foul occurred after the event, it has no effect on which team keeps possession. However, if the foul occurred before the event, and such a penalty is accepted, the down is replayed by the same team that started the previous play on offense.

PERSONAL FOULS

The more serious fouls, including those that might cause injury, are called *personal fouls*, and the guilty team is penalized 15 yards. If a defensive player commits a personal foul, the offense also gets an *automatic first down*. Furthermore, when an official judges that a personal foul was especially severe or flagrant, the guilty player may be *disqualified* (ejected) from the rest of the game. When signaling a personal foul, a referee first gives the hand signal for a personal foul, followed by the signal for the specific foul.

DOUBLE FOULS AND MULTIPLE FOULS

A *double foul* is when opposing teams each commit a foul during the same play or at the same time. The fouls cancel ("offset") each other and the down is replayed from the previous spot. There are two exceptions: (1) if one 15-yard and one 5-yard penalty are called at the same time, the 15-yard penalty is enforced, and the 5-yard penalty is ignored, and (2) on a kicking play where there is a change of possession, the receiving team can choose to either replay the down or keep the ball and take its own penalty as long as its foul occurred after it gained possession.

A *multiple foul* is when players on one team commit more than one foul on a single play. Only one of the penalties can be accepted, and the captain of the non-guilty team chooses which.

LIST OF FOULS
The most common fouls are described below and listed in **Table 1**. The fouls are divided by when they occur during the game: at the beginning of a play, during a play or at anytime. The fouls within each section are listed alphabetically. The first line in each of the descriptions below includes whether the foul is against the offense (Off) or the defense (Def), the amount of penalty yardage for the foul and what spot it should be measured from.

<u>Fouls at the Beginning of a Play</u>
The following fouls occur right before, during or after the snap:

Delay of Game (Off, 5 yds, line of scrimmage) — if the *play clock* expires before the offense snaps the ball. When the *quarterback* sees the play clock winding down and realizes that he might not get the ball snapped in time, he sometimes calls a *time out* to save his team from the penalty.

Encroachment (Off or Def, 5 yds, line of scrimmage) — if a player (besides the *center*) or any part of his body is in the *neutral zone* and contact occurs prior to the snap. The play is not allowed to continue because the foul occurred before the snap (a dead ball foul). Players sometimes end up committing this foul when they are too eager to get a good jump off of the line and accidentally start before the snap.

False Start (Off, 5 yds, line of scrimmage) — if an offensive player *on the line*, after he is *set*, moves in any way that simulates the start of a play, but the ball is not snapped. This is illegal because it misleads defenders into thinking that the play has started. The whistle is blown immediately for this dead ball foul and the play does not count. However, if the offensive player's movement was an immediate reaction to a defensive player entering the neutral zone prior to the snap, a penalty is called against the defense for a *neutral-zone infraction* instead.

Illegal Formation (Off, 5 yds, previous spot) — if an offensive team has fewer than 7 players *on the line* (or within one yard of it) at the time of the snap; also called *illegal procedure.*

Illegal Motion (Off, 5 yds, previous spot)— if an offensive player is moving any part of his body when the ball is snapped. (However, one offensive player in the *backfield*, known as the *man-in-motion*, is permitted to move parallel to the line of scrimmage or away from it before the snap.)

Offside (Off or Def, 5 yds, previous spot) — if a player (besides the center) or any part of his body is beyond his line of scrimmage when the ball is snapped. Any player who gets a head start before the snap has an unfair advantage and is penalized.

Too Many Men on the Field (Off or Def, 5 yds, previous spot) — if a team has more than 11 players on the field when the ball is snapped or an offense has more than 11 in a *huddle*. This foul is not called if the offense purposely snaps the ball quickly to catch the defense with too many players, except in the last 2 minutes of either *half* of an NFL game.

Fouls that Occur During Play
The following fouls usually occur during a play:

Facemask, Incidental (Off or Def, 5 yds, See **Table 3** for spot) — accidentally pulling or twisting an opponent's facemask. Severe or intentional pulling or twisting is considered a personal foul, and is penalized 15 yards.

Holding (Off, 10 yds, previous spot on passing play or See **Table 3** for spot on running play) — if an offensive player impedes the movement of any defender by grasping or hooking any part of the defender's body or uniform with his hands or arms. (See **Figure 22**) (Except when done by a player in an attempt to recover a *loose ball* himself.) This penalty is usually committed when an offensive lineman has no other way to stop an onrushing defender from getting past him.

Figure 22: Holding.

Holding (Def, 5 yds + automatic first down, 10 yds in college, previous spot) — if a defensive player impedes the movement of any offensive player other than the *ball carrier* by grasping or hooking any part of the opponent's body or uniform with his hands or arms. (Except when done by a player in an attempt to recover a loose ball himself.) This penalty is usually committed when a defender tries to inhibit the movement of a pass *receiver* near the line of scrimmage.

Illegal Forward Pass (Off, penalty and spot vary - see below) — A team may make one forward pass and as many *backward passes* (called *laterals*) as it wishes during a play without penalty. It is a foul and an *incomplete pass* if:

- 2 forward passes are thrown during the same play. A 5-yard penalty is assessed from the previous spot.
- a forward pass is thrown from beyond the line of scrimmage. A 5-yard penalty and (in the NFL only) loss of down is assessed against the offense from the spot of the illegal pass.

- a forward pass is thrown from behind the line after the ball has already crossed it once. A 5-yard penalty is assessed from the previous spot.
- a forward pass is completed to an *ineligible receiver*. A 5-yard penalty is assessed from the previous spot.

Illegal Use of Hands (Off, 10 yds, previous spot on passing play or See **Table 3** for spot on running play) — includes:
- an offensive player helps the ball carrier advance by pushing him forward with his hands.
- an offensive player thrusts his hands forward to contact an opponent in the neck, face or head.

Illegal Use of Hands (Def, 5 yds + automatic first down, 10 yds in college, previous spot) — includes these actions:
- a defensive player pushes a pass receiver who is more than 5 yards beyond the line of scrimmage
- a defensive player thrusts his hands forward to contact an opponent in the neck, face or head.

Ineligible Member of Kicking Team Downfield (Off, 5 yds, previous spot) — on a *punt*, if a player on the *kicking team* crosses the line of scrimmage before the ball is kicked. The kick must be re-taken. (Exception: the two *outside linemen* may cross the line early without penalty.) Without this foul, a punter could hold the ball for a while before kicking to give his team's *kick coverage* time to get down the field.

Ineligible Receiver Downfield (Off, 5 yds, previous spot) — on a passing play, if an ineligible receiver, such as an offensive lineman, advances past the line of scrimmage before the ball is passed, except if he got there by *blocking* a defender.

Intentional Grounding (Off, at spot of grounding or 10 yards behind previous spot, whichever is worse, + loss of down) — if the quarterback purposely throws an incomplete forward pass to avoid a *sack*. The penalty is not called if the passer leaves the *pocket* and throws a pass that lands near or beyond the line of scrimmage. Without this rule, a passer about to be *tackled* for a loss of yardage could throw

60

an incomplete pass at the ground or *out of bounds* to assure that the next play starts up at the previous line of scrimmage. Quarterbacks can often avoid this foul by throwing the ball somewhere in the vicinity of a receiver, even if there is no way that the receiver can catch it.

Pass Interference (Off or Def) — if a player impedes an opponent from catching a pass prior to the ball's arrival. (See **Figure 23**) As soon as the pass is touched by any player, contact is allowed. A player also should not be penalized if he accidentally trips or hits an opponent while making a bona fide attempt to catch the ball, or if a pass is thrown too far from a fouled player to be catchable. This foul can be committed by either the offense or defense:

Figure 23: Defensive pass interference.

- Defensive (Def, automatic first down from spot of interference; in college, limited to 15 yds beyond previous spot): This is the more common type of interference because defenders are always trying to prevent receivers from catching passes. Defenders try to make contact with the receiver at the moment the ball arrives (not a penalty) but sometimes get there a little early. If a defender is charged with pass interference in his own end zone, the offense gets a new first down and the ball on the opponent's 1-yard line (2-yard line in college).

- Offensive (Off, 10 yds, 15 yds in college, previous spot): This less-common type of interference usually occurs when a receiver tries to prevent a defender from making an *interception*.

Running into the Kicker (Def, 5 yds, previous spot) — if a defensive player, while trying to block the ball, runs into a *punter* or *place kicker* but is not able to touch the ball. No foul is called against that defender if he touches the ball or has been blocked into the kicker by an offensive player. This penalty can have a big impact on a game, because if an offensive team had less than 5 yards to go for a first down and was punting or trying a field goal on fourth down, the penalty yardage would give it a first down. That team could then continue its offensive *drive*. Tackling or attempting to injure the kicker is a personal foul of *roughing the kicker* (see below).

Personal Fouls that Occur During Play
Listed below are the most common personal fouls. In addition to these, a personal foul can be called against any player who punches, kicks, knees or elbows another player, or against any player who strikes another player in the head, neck or face.

Chop Block (or *Illegal Cut*) (Off, 15 yds, See **Table 3** for spot) — if an offensive player blocks a defensive player below the waist while the latter is already being blocked. (Except when the second blocker was positioned on the line at the start of a running play.) This is illegal because the preoccupied defender has no way to protect his legs from injury.

Clipping (Off or Def, 15 yds + automatic first down if against defense, See **Table 3** for spot) — blocking an opponent from behind below the waist. (Exception: an offensive lineman can block a defensive lineman at the line of scrimmage from behind anywhere above the knees.) Clipping is dangerous because the player being blocked cannot see his blocker to protect himself from possible injury.

Facemask, Flagrant (Off or Def, 15 yds + automatic first down if against defense, See **Table 3** for spot) — intentionally or violently pulling or twisting an opponent's facemask. Incidental grasping of a facemask is not a personal foul, but is still a 5-yard penalty.

Illegal Block Below the Waist (Off or Def, 15 yds + automatic first down if against defense, See **Table 3** for spot) — when any player blocks an opponent below the waist during a *runback* after a *kickoff, punt, safety kick, fumble recovery* or interception.

Roughing the Kicker (Def, 15 yds + automatic first down, previous spot) — A more severe version of Running into the Kicker (see above), where a defender does not merely run into the kicker, but actually hits him hard.

Roughing the Passer (Def, 15 yds + automatic first down, previous spot; in college, succeeding spot if completed pass gains yards) — if a defensive player runs into the passer after the ball has left the passer's hand, or intentionally tries to harm him by driving him into the ground or hitting him with the helmet. A defender is not guilty of running into the passer if the officials judge that he did not have a reasonable chance to stop his momentum. Officials give pass rushers one full step towards the quarterback to stop after the ball has been released.

Unnecessary Roughness (Off or Def, 15 yds + automatic first down if against defense, See **Table 3** for spot) — any action deemed unnecessarily dangerous to another player, including hitting a player who is already out of bounds (called a *late hit*), throwing a runner to the ground after the ball is dead, using the *helmet* as a weapon to ram an opponent (called *spearing*) or falling onto a player after the ball is dead (called *piling on*).

Foul That Can Occur Anytime
Unsportsmanlike Conduct (Off or Def, 15 yds + automatic first down if against defense, succeeding spot) — when a player acts against the spirit of good sportsmanship, including use of abusive language and gestures, taunting, or celebrating too hard in front of the opponent.

Now that we have covered the basics, the next chapter entitled **THINGS TO LOOK FOR DURING PLAY / STRATEGY** will help you to better understand what teams are planning to do before they do it.

THINGS TO LOOK FOR
DURING PLAY / STRATEGY

As a spectator, you will enjoy the game more if you know what to look for when watching a football game. This chapter will help you with two basic parts of being a spectator — following where the ball goes and understanding a team's strategy in choosing to run a particular type of play.

WATCHING THE BALL

To be able to find the ball, you must first know where to look for it. Before each play, the ball lies flat on the ground between the two teams, directly in front of the *center* on the *offense*. You can tell who the center is because the *quarterback* stands right behind him to ask for the *snap*. When the quarterback takes the snap to begin the play, watch him carefully to notice where the ball will go next. In the first 2 or 3 seconds after the snap, you will probably know whether the offense will run or pass.

With a run, the quarterback will immediately hand or *pitch* the ball to a *running back*. Remember to check and see if the running back who you thought was handed the ball actually has it. The quarterback may have faked the *hand-off* and still be holding the ball, ready to pass it *downfield* (called a *play-action pass*). If the quarterback takes several steps backwards immediately after the snap without giving the ball to anyone, prepare to watch him throw the ball forward to a teammate.

VIRTUAL FIRST DOWN LINE

A new television technology has recently made it much easier for you to determine how far a team has to go to earn a *first down* by "painting" a computer-generated bright yellow or orange line right on the field. Now used in all *NFL* and many college football broadcasts, this virtual first down line makes most plays more interesting because you can compare the progress of an offensive player to his objective — a first down. Two American companies — Sportvision and Princeton Video Image — have developed similar video overlay technologies that use multiple high-speed computers to integrate the graphic into the broadcast on the fly and make the illusion seem real.

CHOOSING AN OFFENSIVE PLAY
When a team is *on offense*, it weighs several different factors in choosing a play — what *down* it is, how many yards it needs for a first down, its *field position*, the *score* of the game and the amount of time remaining. Many times, you can guess what the next play will be merely by knowing the situation. Other times, the offense will do the opposite of what is expected to catch the defense, who is also guessing, off-guard. The following discussion explains why a team chooses certain types of plays in various situations.

<u>Running Play vs. Passing Play</u>
In general, a *passing play* is a higher risk method of advancing the ball than a *running play*, but it also provides greater rewards. In the NFL, the average running play gains about 4 yards compared to a gain of about 12 yards for the average completed pass. However, far more things can go wrong on a passing play. Since fewer than 60% of all passes attempted are even completed (called a *completion percentage*), over 40% of passes are *incomplete* and waste a down with no yardage gain. Worse yet, the *quarterback* is sometimes *sacked*, losing yards for the offense, or the ball is *intercepted* and the offense loses *possession* of the ball. When things go right, though, the payoff is usually much greater than a running play. Most long gains and the majority of *touchdowns* are on passing plays.

A coach considers these averages when choosing a play. When a team needs less than 3 or 4 yards for a first down, called a *short yardage situation*, he will often call for a run. However, when it needs more than 5 yards in a single play, such as in a third-and-10 or third-and-8 situation (also called *third-and-long*), he almost always calls for a passing play designed to get the ball to an *open receiver* beyond the *necessary line*. When no clear short or *long yardage situation* exists, the coach usually chooses the type of play that best utilizes his team's talent. For example, the Pittsburgh Steelers prefer running plays because they have bruising running back Jerome Bettis, while the St. Louis Rams attempt more passing plays because they have one of the NFL's best quarterbacks in *Kurt Warner*.

A running or passing play is also chosen to *control the game clock* late in the game. A team on offense that needs to score quickly, such as one losing with time running out, will choose mostly passing plays because they conserve time. This team can throw all of its passes towards the *sidelines* so that receivers can catch the ball and quickly get *out of bounds* to stop the clock. If a quarterback cannot find a receiver, he can still stop the clock by throwing an incomplete pass. He can also stop it by deliberately throwing the ball to the ground, or *spiking* it, immediatle after receiving the snap.

By contrast, on a running play, the only way to stop the clock is for the *ball carrier* to run across a sideline to get out of bounds, a more difficult task. If this player were to be tackled in bounds, the clock would continue to tick down and a team might be forced to use one of its precious *time outs*. However, running plays are ideal for an offense that has the lead late in the game and is trying to waste clock time. This team can call one running play after another and the clock will continue to run down unless the defense calls a time out.

Fourth Down Situations: Punt, Field Goal, or Go For It
When an offensive team faces a *fourth down*, its play selection is crucial because if it does not make enough yards to get a first down, it loses possession of the ball. Its options are as follows: it can *punt* the ball to the other team, attempt a *field goal* or try to gain the necessary yards for a first down to keep possession (called *going for it*).

Normally, a team will not go for it on fourth down within its own *territory* (its own side of the 50-yard line), even if it only needs an inch for a first down, because if it does not make it, the opponent gets the ball in good field position. Instead, most teams in this situation choose to punt, giving away possession of the ball in return for pushing the opponent back into poorer field position. The punting team then relies on its *defensive unit* to stop the opponents and regain possession of the ball. One exception to this is when a team is losing with time running out. On fourth down, this team would probably choose to go for it even from deep in its own territory because its only chance to win the game is to make the necessary yardage and continue its *drive* towards a score.

When an offense is in its opponent's territory, its fourth-down strategy is less clear. Inside the opponent's 30-yard line, the offense might try to kick a field goal to score 3 points because it has a reasonable chance of making it from that distance (it is in *field goal range*). However, if a team is losing by more than 3 points late in the game and needs a touchdown, or has such a small distance to go that it believes its chances of getting the first down are very high, it will go for a first down even when a field goal would be easy.

Outside the opponent's 30-yard line, only teams with *place kickers* that can make long field goals will attempt to kick one. A rule adopted by the NFL in 1994 deters even these teams from trying such long field goals. This rule gives the defense better field position after a missed kick by placing the ball at the spot of the kick instead of the *previous line of scrimmage*, a 7 yard difference (in college the ball is still placed at the previous line of scrimmage.) Instead, offenses facing a fourth down between the opponent's 30- and 50-yard lines often will either punt the ball to try to pin the defense deep in its own territory or go for a first down. Going for the first down is not as risky from this area because even if the offense does not make it, the opponent is still in its own territory when it regains possession.

The next chapter entitled **FORMATIONS AND PLAYS** introduces specific plays and how teams use them.

FORMATIONS AND PLAYS

At the beginning of each play, *offensive* and *defensive* players arrange themselves in a pattern called a *formation* or a *set*. Teams use different formations to make it easier to attempt particular types of plays. This chapter explores the common formations teams use and the various types of plays they run from these formations.

OFFENSIVE FORMATIONS
The rules of football require that there be at least 7 offensive players *on the line* when the ball is *snapped* or the *officials* call an *illegal formation foul* against the *offense*. Once an offensive team sets up in its formation before the snap, it is forbidden to move except for a single *man-in-motion* (although any offensive player may slowly move his head or shoulders). If it needs to adjust to an unexpected *defensive formation*, it is the *quarterback*'s duty to alter the play by calling an *audible* at the *line of scrimmage*. The following is a list of some of the most commonly-used *offensive formations* (See **Figure 24**):

I-Formation — Two *running backs* line up directly behind the quarterback, forming an "I". Teams often use the "I" for *running plays* because the *backs* are close enough to the quarterback to easily take a *hand-off* and the *fullback* is in a good position to *block* for the *halfback*. In the "I", the halfback is also called the *tailback*.

Split Formation — Two running backs line up behind and a few yards to each side of the quarterback. This formation is versatile, good for either a run or pass. The backs can easily get the ball from the quarterback and help *block* for him on *passing plays*.

Spread Formation — The two running backs line up right behind the line just outside the *left* and *right tackles*. This formation is usually used to launch passing plays because it allows the running backs to get off the line more easily so they can act as 4th and 5th *receivers* (joining the two *wide receivers* and the *tight end*).

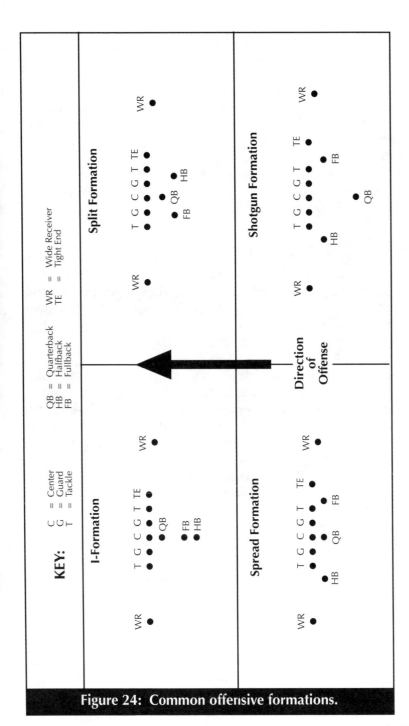

Figure 24: Common offensive formations.

69

Shotgun Formation — This is the same as the spread formation except the quarterback waits for the snap several yards behind the line. Popularized by the *Dallas Cowboys* in the 1970s, the shotgun is used on passing plays to give the quarterback more time to find *open* receivers because he does not waste any time back-pedaling into a passing position.

OFFENSIVE PLAYS

There are dozens of different offensive plays scripted by coaches. Here are some of the plays that you as a spectator should learn to recognize:

Running Plays
Draw Play — The quarterback *drops back* as if to pass, but hands-off to a running back after a split-second delay. This hesitation gives the *defensive linemen* time to *penetrate* the line of scrimmage where *offensive linemen* are waiting to block them out of the way, *clearing a hole* for the running back to dart through.

Reverse / Double Reverse — A quarterback takes the snap, runs in one direction and hands the ball to a teammate traveling in the opposite direction. The new ball carrier scampers around the back side of his line, emerging at the other side of the field. This play is effective because defenders following the quarterback have difficulty changing directions to catch the reversing player. A less common play is the double reverse, where the first reversing player hands-off to yet another offensive player running in the same direction the quarterback originally had been running.

Sweep — A running back takes a hand-off and follows *pulling* offensive linemen around one end of the line. The play is designed to provide a wall of blockers for the runner so he has time to get around the outside of the defense.

Passing Plays
Bomb — A long pass thrown to a receiver sprinting down the field. The chances of success are low because the timing of the quarterback and receiver must be perfect, but if it

works, the offense can gain 50 or more yards in one play and maybe score a *touchdown*. The bomb works best when the defense does not expect it and assigns only one defender for the receiver to *beat* (called *single coverage*).

Flea Flicker — A *trick play* to fool the defense, where the quarterback hands the ball off to a running back who runs towards the line as if it were a running play. When he gets there, however, he *pitches* the ball back to the quarterback who passes to receivers *downfield*. The deception works if defenders come to the line to *tackle* the runner, leaving receivers open behind them.

Play-Action Pass — The quarterback fakes a hand-off to a running back, then drops back to pass. Offensive linemen join in the deception by acting as if they are *run blocking*, drawing defenders who anticipate a running play up to the line. This leaves space in the *defensive backfield* for receivers to get open and catch passes.

Screen Pass — A short pass thrown over onrushing defenders to a running back or receiver. This is especially effective when several defenders have already penetrated the line of scrimmage, such as on a *blitz* (described below).

Option Plays
An offensive player runs with the ball behind the line of scrimmage, trying to find an open receiver to pass to. If he cannot, he has the option of keeping the ball himself to try to gain yards. There are *quarterback options*, where the quarterback takes the snap and *rolls out* (runs parallel to the line), and *halfback options*, where the halfback takes a hand-off or pitch from the quarterback and does the same thing.

Option plays keep the defense off-balance because it does not know whether the *ball carrier* will run or pass until the last moment. They are far more common in college football where less sophisticated defenses have more difficulty stopping them.

DEFENSIVE FORMATIONS

Different defensive formations prepare a team to stop various offensive plays. The two basic formations are the *4-3 defense* and the *3-4 defense,* and a team usually chooses one of these and sticks with it for the entire game. The other formations are used during the game in more specialized situations. The following is a list of some of the most commonly-used defensive formations (See **Figure 25**):

4-3 Defense — 4 defensive linemen on the line with 3 linebackers behind them; the other 4 players are defensive backs. More NFL teams use this formation today than any other. The 4-3 defends well against running plays and makes for a strong pass rush because it places 4 men on the line. However, having only 3 linebackers reduces the defense's ability to cover receivers on passing plays.

3-4 Defense — 3 defensive linemen on the line with 4 *linebackers* behind them; the other 4 players are *defensive backs.* The 4 linebackers can move forward to stop running plays or drop back to *cover* receivers on passing plays. This used to be the most commonly-used defensive formation in the 1980s because it is the most flexible, but most of today's teams prefer the extra pressure a fourth lineman places on the quarterback in the 4-3.

Nickel or *Dime Defense* — A nickel defense is any formation where a 5th defensive back, called the nickel back, replaces a linebacker on the field. A dime defense is where two nickel backs, the 5th and 6th defensive backs, replace linebackers. A defense brings in these extra defensive backs to increase its *pass coverage* when it is likely that the opponent will call a passing play such as on *third-and-long.* However, these formations take defenders away from the front line, making the defense more vulnerable to running plays.

Goal Line Defense — A defense with its back against its own *goal line* often places 6 or more players on the line to prevent the offense from running the ball into the *end zone* for a touchdown. The lack of defenders in the defensive backfield leaves the defense vulnerable to passing plays.

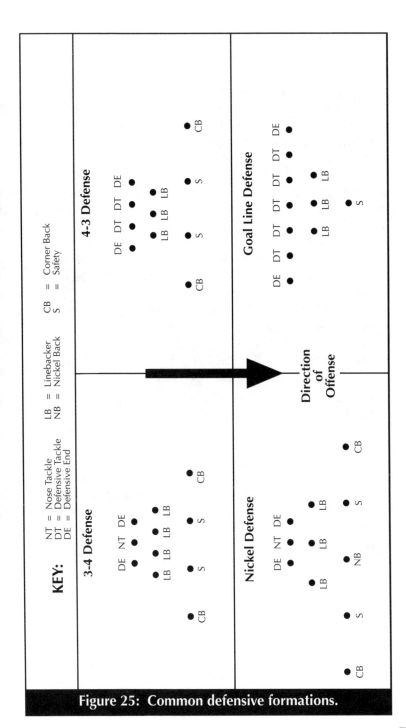

KEY: NT = Nose Tackle LB = Linebacker CB = Corner Back
DT = Defensive Tackle NB = Nickel Back S = Safety
DE = Defensive End

3-4 Defense

4-3 Defense

Nickel Defense

Goal Line Defense

Direction
of
Offense

Figure 25: Common defensive formations.

DEFENSIVE PLAYS

The most common types of defensive plays are:

Zone Defense — Each linebacker and defensive back is assigned to a particular area of the defensive backfield, covering any receiver who enters it. When the ball is thrown into a *zone*, players from nearby zones move quickly to help the primary defender of that zone. This defense allows more short passes to be completed in front of or between the zones, but tends to prevent receivers from making long gains after catching the ball by having defenders help each other in tackling the receivers.

Man-to-Man Defense — Each linebacker and defensive back is assigned to cover a particular offensive player to prevent him from catching passes. The assignments are usually as follows:

- Linebackers cover the running backs
- *Cornerbacks* cover the wide receivers
- One *safety*, called the *strong safety*, covers the tight end
- Another safety, called the *free safety*, roams the field and is available to help the other defenders

Fewer passes are completed against the man-to-man defense because coverage is tighter, but if a receiver beats his defender, there may be no other player to stop the receiver from going all the way for a touchdown.

Blitz / Dog — A blitz begins as soon as the ball is snapped when a defensive team sends defensive backs and linebackers rushing towards the line of scrimmage to try to break through and *sack* the quarterback. A dog is a blitz carried out solely by a team's linebackers. Even if blitzing defenders do not tackle the quarterback, they try to make him hurry his pass, often forcing him to throw an *incomplete pass* or an *interception*.

Prevent Defense — A team playing in a nickel or dime formation concedes short gains to the offense in exchange for preventing a long gain. Coaches whose teams are winning late in a game often use this strategy thinking that the offense will use up more time by making a series of short gains. However, defenders playing a prevent defense often give the offense too much room to operate, allowing it to score more quickly than it would against normal defensive pressure.

SPECIAL TEAMS PLAYS

Special types of *kicking plays* may help teams win games:

Fake Punt / Fake Field Goal — The offense lines up on *fourth down* as if it is going to punt or attempt a field goal, but instead goes for a *first down*. On most fakes, the *punter* (on punts) or the *holder* (on field goals) takes the snap and either runs with it or passes it to a receiver. While a team that is losing may need a successful fake punt or field goal to maintain possession of the ball, the fake is more successful when it can catch the defense by surprise. Most teams attempt fakes from near *midfield* since an unsuccessful fake from deep in their own *territory* would leave their opponents with excellent *field position*.

Onside Kick — On a *kickoff*, the ball is kicked short so the kicking team can try and *recover* it before the receiving team. Since a kickoff is a *loose ball*, whichever team recovers the ball first gets to keep it. However, the kicking team is penalized if it touches the ball before the kick has traveled forward 10 yards (unless an opponent touched the ball first) — this prevents a kicker from tapping the ball directly to a teammate. In the NFL, the kicking team must re-kick the ball from 5 yards further back. A repeat offense in the NFL or any instance of this violation in a college game gives the ball to the receiving team where the ball was illegally touched.

With most onside kicks, the kicker bounces a short kick along the ground, hoping the ball takes an unpredictable hop which allows his teammates to recover it. Onside kicks are usually used by teams that need to regain possession of the ball quickly because they are behind in the score late in the game. They are used sparingly, though, because if the receiving team recovers the short kick, it gets the ball in excellent field position.

The next section will help you learn about **DECIPHERING FOOTBALL STATISTICS.**

DECIPHERING FOOTBALL STATISTICS

Football performance on the field is measured by a seemingly endless array of numbers, averages and percentages. Some statistics measure the performance of individual players while others gauge the play of teams. This chapter introduces these statistics and explains how they are measured.

INDIVIDUAL PASSING STATISTICS

These are most often kept for *quarterbacks (QB)*. Below are the 2001 statistics for St. Louis Rams' quarterback *Kurt Warner*:

Player	Att	Comp	Pct	Yds	TD	Int	Long	Rating
Warner	546	375	68.7	4830	36	22	65t	101.4

These numbers tell us the following about Warner's season:

Att — *Passing Attempts*: # of times he threw a *forward pass*.

Comp — Pass Completions: # of his passes completed to a teammate.

Pct — *Completion Percentage*: % of the passes he attempted that were complete (= **Comp** / **Att**). (Warner is a very accurate passer, over 10% above the league average of 58%.)

Yds — *Passing Yardage*: Gross yards gained on all plays he threw a *forward pass*. (Warner's 4,830 yards passing was the second-best total in NFL history. Average QBs throw for 3,000 yds.)

TD — *Touchdown Passes*: # of times he threw a pass that was caught by a *receiver* who scored a touchdown. (Warner was the league leader, well above the *NFL* average of 18.)

Int — *Interceptions*: # of his passes intercepted by an opponent. Good QBs throw more TDs than Int, as Warner did.

Long — Longest Pass Completion: Longest distance in yards gained on a single pass thrown by Warner (the "t" indicates it was a touchdown).

Rating — *Passer Rating*: A number indicating the overall success of a passer, calculated by a complicated formula. A rating of 75 is average, and 90 or better is considered excellent.

INDIVIDUAL RUSHING STATISTICS

These are most often kept for *running backs (RB)*. Below are the 2001 statistics for St. Louis Rams' running back *Marshall Faulk*:

Player	Att	Yds	Avg	Long	TD
Faulk	260	1382	5.3	71t	12

These numbers tell us the following about Faulk's season:

Att — *Rushing Attempts*: # of plays he ran with the ball.

Yds — *Rushing Yardage*: Net yards measured from the *line of scrimmage* on all plays he carried the ball. (Faulk had the fifth-best total that season — an average running back gains 800-1,000 yards.)

Avg — *Average Gain*: Average distance in yards he gained when he ran with the ball (= **Yds** / **Att**). (Faulk had the best in the NFL, well above the league average of 4.1.)

Long — Long Gain: His longest gain on a rushing attempt (the "t" indicates it was a touchdown).

TD — *Rushing Touchdowns*: # of times he took a *hand-off* or *lateral* and crossed the opponent's *goal line*. (Faulk was tied for second in the NFL in this category.)

INDIVIDUAL RECEIVING STATISTICS

These are most often kept for *wide receivers (WR)* and *tight ends*. Below are the 2001 statistics for Minnesota Vikings' wide receiver *Randy Moss*:

Player	No.	Yds	Avg	Long	TD
Moss	82	1233	15.0	73t	10

These numbers tell us the following about Moss' season:

No. — *Receptions*: # of times he caught a forward pass. (Moss had an average number of receptions.)

Yds — *Receiving Yardage*: Net yards measured from the line of scrimmage on all plays he caught a forward pass.

Avg — Average Gain: Average distance in yards he gained when he caught a forward pass (= **Yds** / **No.**). (Moss usually catches passes longer than the NFL average of 11.6 yds.)

Long — Long Gain: Longest gain by Moss on a reception (the "t" indicates it was a touchdown).

TD — *Touchdown Receptions*: # of times Moss scored a touchdown after catching a pass. (Only 3 players had more. Most starting WRs catch between 5 and 9.)

OTHER INDIVIDUAL OFFENSIVE STATISTICS

The following statistics are seen on TV and in the newspaper:

Field Goal Attempts (FGA) — # of *field goals* attempted by a kicker.

Field Goals (FG) — # of field goals made by a kicker.

Extra Points Attempted (XPA) and Made (XP) — # of *point-after-touchdowns* attempted and made by a kicker.

Total Points (Pts.) — # of points physically scored by any player. Just like teams, players get 6 points for scoring a TD, 3 for kicking a field goal, and 1 for kicking an extra point. A passer does not earn points for throwing a TD pass. Most top scorers are kickers because they get so many FGAs.

Gross Punting Average (Gross Avg.) — Average number of yards of a *punter's* *punts*, measured from the line of scrimmage to where the opposition first gains *possession*. A *net punting average* subtracts the *return average* from the gross.

Return Average — Average number of yards gained by a *kickoff* or *punt returner* from where he gains possession.

INDIVIDUAL DEFENSIVE STATISTICS

Interceptions — # of passes intercepted by a player.

Sacks — # of times a player *tackled* the quarterback for a loss of yards. If 2 players combine for a sack, each gets $\frac{1}{2}$ credit.

TEAM STATISTICS

Win-Loss-Tie Record — # of games a team has won, lost and tied. For example, a 10-5-1 record means a team has won 10 games, lost 5 and tied 1.

First Downs — # of times a team gained 10 yards in 4 or less plays.

3rd Down Efficiency — % of the time that a team facing a third down earns a first down on that play.

Turnovers — # of times a team lost a *fumble* or threw an interception.

Penalties, Yards — # of penalties assessed against a team and the total # of yards it was penalized.

Time of Possession — Amount of cumulative time, measured by the *game clock*, that a team was *on offense*. The longer a team has possession, the more chance it has to score.

READING A GAME SUMMARY

Being able to understand a *game summary* or *boxscore* in the daily newspaper allows a reader to re-create the action and sequence of events that took place during a football game. The various pieces of information contained in a game summary are explained below:

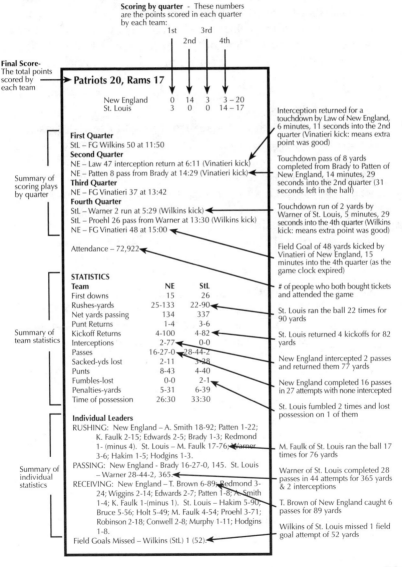

Scoring by quarter - These numbers are the points scored in each quarter by each team:
1st
2nd
3rd
4th

Final Score- The total points scored by each team

> **Patriots 20, Rams 17**

	1st	2nd	3rd	4th	
New England	0	14	3	3	– 20
St. Louis	3	0	0	14	– 17

Summary of scoring plays by quarter

First Quarter
StL – FG Wilkins 50 at 11:50
Second Quarter
NE – Law 47 interception return at 6:11 (Vinatieri kick)
NE – Patten 8 pass from Brady at 14:29 (Vinatieri kick)
Third Quarter
NE – FG Vinatieri 37 at 13:42
Fourth Quarter
StL – Warner 2 run at 5:29 (Wilkins kick)
StL – Proehl 26 pass from Warner at 13:30 (Wilkins kick)
NE – FG Vinatieri 48 at 15:00

Attendance – 72,922

Interception returned for a touchdown by Law of New England, 6 minutes, 11 seconds into the 2nd quarter (Vinatieri kick: means extra point was good)

Touchdown pass of 8 yards completed from Brady to Patten of New England, 14 minutes, 29 seconds into the 2nd quarter (31 seconds left in the half)

Touchdown run of 2 yards by Warner of St. Louis, 5 minutes, 29 seconds into the 4th quarter (Wilkins kick: means extra point was good)

Field Goal of 48 yards kicked by Vinatieri of New England, 15 minutes into the 4th quarter (as the game clock expired)

# of people who both bought tickets and attended the game

Summary of team statistics

STATISTICS

Team	NE	StL
First downs	15	26
Rushes-yards	25-133	22-90
Net yards passing	134	337
Punt Returns	1-4	3-6
Kickoff Returns	4-100	4-82
Interceptions	2-77	0-0
Passes	16-27-0	28-44-2
Sacked-yds lost	2-11	5-28
Punts	8-43	4-40
Fumbles-lost	0-0	2-1
Penalties-yards	5-31	6-39
Time of possession	26:30	33:30

St. Louis ran the ball 22 times for 90 yards

St. Louis returned 4 kickoffs for 82 yards

New England intercepted 2 passes and returned them 77 yards

New England completed 16 passes in 27 attempts with none intercepted

St. Louis fumbled 2 times and lost possession on 1 of them

Summary of individual statistics

Individual Leaders
RUSHING: New England – A. Smith 18-92; Patten 1-22; K. Faulk 2-15; Edwards 2-5; Brady 1-3; Redmond 1- (minus 4). St. Louis – M. Faulk 17-76; Warner 3-6; Hakim 1-5; Hodgins 1-3.
PASSING: New England - Brady 16-27-0, 145. St. Louis – Warner 28-44-2, 365.
RECEIVING: New England – T. Brown 6-89; Redmond 3-24; Wiggins 2-14; Edwards 2-7; Patten 1-8; A. Smith 1-4; K. Faulk 1-(minus 1). St. Louis – Hakim 5-90; Bruce 5-56; Holt 5-49; M. Faulk 4-54; Proehl 3-71; Robinson 2-18; Conwell 2-8; Murphy 1-11; Hodgins 1-8.
Field Goals Missed – Wilkins (StL) 1 (52).

M. Faulk of St. Louis ran the ball 17 times for 76 yards

Warner of St. Louis completed 28 passes in 44 attempts for 365 yards & 2 interceptions

T. Brown of New England caught 6 passes for 89 yards

Wilkins of St. Louis missed 1 field goal attempt of 52 yards

NFL TEAMS, DIVISIONS and CONFERENCES

The *NFL* consists of 32 teams evenly divided into 2 *conferences* — the *National Football Conference* (*NFC*) and the *American Football Conference* (*AFC*). Each conference is further broken into 4 *divisions* — the *Eastern, Northern, Southern* and *Western Divisions*. Before the 2002 season, each conference, which previously had only 3 divisions (Eastern, *Central*, Western), added a fourth division and *realigned* several teams to fill it. All of the NFL teams (*franchises*) are listed by division on the next page.

GROWTH OF THE NFL

Only 3 original teams remain from the NFL's first season in 1922 — the Chicago Bears (originally from Decatur, Illinois), the Arizona Cardinals (from Chicago) and the Green Bay Packers. Dozens of teams played in the NFL during its first 30 years, but only 12 remained by 1953. Since then, every team that has played in the NFL is still playing today, though many have moved. In the 1960s, the NFL added 4 teams through *expansion*, plus 10 more when it merged with the *American Football League* (*AFL*) in 1970, for a total of 26 teams.

RECENT EXPANSION

Between 1968 and 1994, only 2 teams were added to the NFL, when the Tampa Bay Buccaneers and the Seattle Seahawks joined the league in 1976, bringing it to 28 teams. These teams were painfully overmatched their first few years, especially Tampa Bay which lost its first 26 games in a row. The first expansion in 20 years added 2 more teams to the NFL in 1995 — the Carolina Panthers and the Jacksonville Jaguars. These teams fared far better than their expansion predecessors, both making it to the conference championship games in 1996 in only their second season.

In 1999, the NFL added an expansion team for Cleveland, resurrecting the legendary Browns who moved to Baltimore in 1996. Further expansion in 2002 brought the new Houston Texans to the city that lost its Oilers to Tennessee in 1997.

Key: *APFA = American Professional Football Association*
AAFC = All-American Football Conference
AFL = American Football League
Footnotes indicate most recent franchise relocations

	Established	Came From	Prior Locations and Years
American Conference			
Eastern Division			
Buffalo Bills	1960	AFL	
Miami Dolphins	1966	AFL	
New England Patriots	1960	AFL	Boston (1960-70)
New York Jets	1960	AFL	
Northern Division			
Baltimore Ravens[1]	1946	AAFC	Cleveland (1946-95)
Cincinnati Bengals	1968	AFL	
Cleveland Browns[2]	1999	NFL	
Pittsburgh Steelers	1933	NFL	
Southern Division			
Houston Texans	2002	NFL	
Indianapolis Colts[3]	1953	NFL	Baltimore (1953-83)
Jacksonville Jaguars	1995	NFL	
Tennessee Titans[4]	1960	AFL	Houston (1960-96)
Western Division			
Denver Broncos	1960	AFL	
Kansas City Chiefs	1960	AFL	Dallas (1960-62)
Oakland Raiders[5]	1960	AFL	Los Angeles (1982-94)
San Diego Chargers	1960	AFL	Los Angeles (1960)
National Conference			
Eastern Division			
Dallas Cowboys	1960	NFL	
New York Giants	1925	NFL	
Philadelphia Eagles	1933	NFL	
Washington Redskins	1932	NFL	Boston (1932-36)
Northern Division			
Chicago Bears	1920	APFA	Decatur, Illinois (1920)
Detroit Lions	1930	NFL	Portsmouth, OH (1930-33)
Green Bay Packers	1921	APFA	
Minnesota Vikings	1961	NFL	
Southern Division			
Atlanta Falcons	1966	NFL	
Carolina Panthers	1995	NFL	
New Orleans Saints	1967	NFL	
Tampa Bay Buccaneers	1976	NFL	
Western Division			
Arizona Cardinals[6]	1920	APFA	Chicago (1920-59), St. Louis (1960-87)
St. Louis Rams[7]	1937	NFL	Cleveland (1937-45) Los Angeles (1946-79) Anaheim (1980-94)
San Francisco 49ers	1946	AAFC	
Seattle Seahawks	1976	NFL	

[1] were Cleveland Browns through 1995 season
[2] 1999 expansion team; the original Cleveland Browns moved to Baltimore in 1996 to become the Ravens
[3] were Baltimore Colts through 1983 season
[4] were Houston Oilers through 1996 season; changed name from Tennessee Oilers in 1999
[5] were Oakland Raiders through 1981 season, then Los Angeles Raiders through 1994 season
[6] were St. Louis Cardinals through 1987 season; changed name from Phoenix Cardinals in 1994
[7] were Los Angeles Rams through 1994 season

NFL SEASON, PLAYOFFS
and THE SUPER BOWL

Every year, *NFL* teams compete to earn the chance to play in the most-watched sporting event in America — the *Super Bowl*. It takes nearly 6 months to decide which teams reach this championship game of professional football, including the *pre-season*, the *regular season* and the *playoffs*.

PRE-SEASON
During the month of August, before football's regular season begins, teams play games against one another to practice plays in realistic situations and decide which players belong on their final *rosters*. Each team plays 4 pre-season (*exhibition*) games using the regular rules of football, but the results of the games are not counted in the *standings*. In addition to games played in NFL stadiums, each season one pre-season game called the *American Bowl* is played at an international site such as Tokyo, Barcelona, Sydney or Mexico City to expose citizens of other countries to the excitement of American football.

REGULAR SEASON
The NFL's regular season lasts from early September to late December, during which each team plays 16 weekly games to try to qualify for the *post-season* tournament called the playoffs. Most of the week's games are played on Sunday and one on Monday night. Since 1990, each team has been given 1 or 2 off-weeks per season during which it is not scheduled to play, called a *bye* week. This has extended the season to either 17 or 18 weeks.

The opponent a team faces each week is determined by a schedule drawn up soon after the previous season has ended. Of the 16 games a team plays, it faces each team in its *division* twice, once at home and once on the road. This is called a *home-and-home series* and it helps promote rivalries among teams in the same division. With the realignment of NFL teams into eight 4-team divisions in 2002, a new scheduling format also ensures that every team meets every other NFL team at least once every 4 years. A team's success is measured by its *record* in *wins*, *losses* and *ties* during the regular season, giving it a *winning percentage* calculated as follows:

$$\text{Winning Percentage} = \frac{\#\text{wins} + (\#\text{ties}/2)}{\#\text{games played}}$$

QUALIFYING FOR THE PLAYOFFS

Twelve of the NFL's 32 teams qualify for the playoffs each year. The team with the best record in each of the 8 divisions is called the *division champion* and automatically qualifies for the playoffs. In addition, 4 more teams, those with the 2 best records in each *conference* that were not division champions, also qualify for the playoffs as *Wild Card* teams.

If two or more teams trying to make the playoffs are tied with the same record, *tie-breakers* are used to determine which team(s) qualifies. To break a tie, the teams are compared first on the basis of their record in head-to-head competition, then on their record in division games (to determine a division champion) or conference games (to determine a Wild Card), their record in games with common opponents and *net points* (points scored minus points allowed).

The location of each playoff game is also determined by the regular-season finish of the participating teams. Division champions always get to play at home against Wild Card teams (called *home field advantage*), and when division champions or Wild Card teams play among themselves, home field advantage is given to the team with the better record. Therefore, the team with the best record in its conference plays at home as long as it lasts in the playoffs until the Super Bowl. If two competing teams have the same record, the playoff tie-breakers listed above are also used to determine the home team.

THE NFL PLAYOFFS

The week after the regular season ends, the NFL playoffs begin. The playoffs are a *single-elimination* tournament where the winner of each game advances to the next game and the loser goes on vacation until the next season. (See **Figure 26**) The first week of the playoffs is the *Wild Card Round*. In each conference, the 2 division champions with the worst record play at home against the 2 Wild Card teams. The 2 division champions with the best records get a *bye*.

The second round of the playoffs called the *Divisional Playoffs* is played the following week. In each conference, the division champion with the best record hosts the team with the worst record that survived the first round, and the division champion with the second-best record plays the other winner of the Wild Card Round. The 2 winners of the Divisional Playoffs in each conference play each other the following week in the Conference Championship Games to determine the AFC and NFC Champions who then advance to the *Super Bowl*.

THE SUPER BOWL

Normally played in late January, the Super Bowl is held at a neutral site determined years before the game is actually played. It is always chosen to be at a warm-weather location or an indoor stadium to avoid having winter weather interfere with the competition. An extra week off between the Conference Championship Games and the Super Bowl is sometimes included in the schedule to allow the teams more time to prepare for the big game and to let the suspense and media hype build.

Certainly the Super Bowl needs no more hype than it already attracts. The Top 5 most-watched television shows in history are all recent Super Bowls, each seen by over 130 million people in the U.S. alone, not to mention an estimated 800 million fans in 180 other countries.

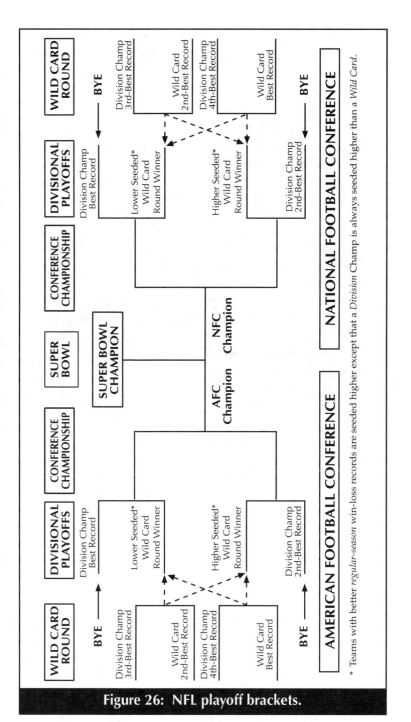

Figure 26: NFL playoff brackets.

85

Although the first championship between football's American and National Conferences was played after the 1966 season in January 1967, it was not until the January 1969 championship that the game was dubbed the Super Bowl. Since that was the third championship played, it was called Super Bowl III and historians retroactively named the 1967 game Super Bowl I. Listed in **Table 4** below is a record of every Super Bowl played through Super Bowl XXXVI in January 2002 (the championship of the 2001 season). Notice how the Super Bowl is played in January of the year *after* the entire regular season.

THE NFL ON TELEVISION

You should have no problem finding NFL action on television during the season, with 3 broadcast networks and a cable network showing games. In 1998, the NFL negotiated the richest television rights agreements of any sport in history, providing it with $18 billion over 8 years for the rights to broadcast games through the 2005 season. These higher revenues automatically triggered an increase in the *salary cap* that all teams operate under, allowing them to dole out higher pay to the players.

In this 1998 bidding contest, CBS regained NFL football by winning the rights to show AFC games just 4 years after it lost the NFC to Fox in a 1994 bidding war. Fox retained the NFC games, while ABC continued to broadcast the ever-popular *Monday Night Football*. ESPN won the rights to broadcast the entire season of Sunday Night games it had earlier split with TNT, while NBC was left without any rights to televise the NFL.

Every Sunday, local network affiliates choose the games which they believe will be of highest interest to their viewers. To encourage fan attendance in cities with NFL teams, networks are forbidden from showing home games unless the games are sold out, called a *blackout*.

Super Bowl *	Year **	Winner	Loser	Score	Location
I	1967	Green Bay Packers	Kansas City Chiefs	35-10	Memorial Coliseum, Los Angeles
II	1968	Green Bay Packers	Oakland Raiders	33-14	Orange Bowl, Miami
III	1969	New York Jets	Baltimore Colts	16-7	Orange Bowl, Miami
IV	1970	Kansas City Chiefs	Minnesota Vikings	23-7	Tulane Stadium, New Orleans
V	1971	Baltimore Colts	Dallas Cowboys	16-13	Orange Bowl, Miami
VI	1972	Dallas Cowboys	Miami Dolphins	24-3	Tulane Stadium, New Orleans
VII	1973	Miami Dolphins	Washington Redskins	14-7	Memorial Coliseum, Los Angeles
VIII	1974	Miami Dolphins	Minnesota Vikings	24-7	Rice Stadium, Houston
IX	1975	Pittsburgh Steelers	Minnesota Vikings	16-6	Tulane Stadium, New Orleans
X	1976	Pittsburgh Steelers	Dallas Cowboys	21-17	Orange Bowl, Miami
XI	1977	Oakland Raiders	Minnesota Vikings	32-14	Rose Bowl, Pasadena
XII	1978	Dallas Cowboys	Denver Broncos	27-10	Superdome, New Orleans
XIII	1979	Pittsburgh Steelers	Dallas Cowboys	35-31	Orange Bowl, Miami
XIV	1980	Pittsburgh Steelers	Los Angeles Rams	31-19	Rose Bowl, Pasadena
XV	1981	Oakland Raiders	Philadelphia Eagles	27-10	Superdome, New Orleans
XVI	1982	San Francisco 49ers	Cincinnati Bengals	26-21	Silverdome, Pontiac
XVII	1983	Washington Redskins	Miami Dolphins	27-17	Rose Bowl, Pasadena
XVIII	1984	Los Angeles Raiders	Washington Redskins	38-9	Tampa Stadium, Tampa
XIX	1985	San Francisco 49ers	Miami Dolphins	38-16	Stanford Stadium, Stanford
XX	1986	Chicago Bears	New England Patriots	46-10	Superdome, New Orleans
XXI	1987	New York Giants	Denver Broncos	39-20	Rose Bowl, Pasadena
XXII	1988	Washington Redskins	Denver Broncos	42-10	Jack Murphy Stadium, San Diego
XXIII	1989	San Francisco 49ers	Cincinnati Bengals	20-16	Joe Robbie Stadium, Miami
XXIV	1990	San Francisco 49ers	Denver Broncos	55-10	Superdome, New Orleans
XXV	1991	New York Giants	Buffalo Bills	20-19	Tampa Stadium, Tampa
XXVI	1992	Washington Redskins	Buffalo Bills	37-24	Metrodome, Minneapolis
XXVII	1993	Dallas Cowboys	Buffalo Bills	52-17	Rose Bowl, Pasadena
XXVIII	1994	Dallas Cowboys	Buffalo Bills	30-13	Georgia Dome, Atlanta
XXIX	1995	San Francisco 49ers	San Diego Chargers	49-26	Joe Robbie Stadium, Miami
XXX	1996	Dallas Cowboys	Pittsburgh Steelers	27-17	Sun Devil Stadium, Tempe, Arizona
XXXI	1997	Green Bay Packers	New England Patriots	35-21	Superdome, New Orleans
XXXII	1998	Denver Broncos	Green Bay Packers	31-24	Jack Murphy Stadium, San Diego
XXXIII	1999	Denver Broncos	Atlanta Falcons	34-19	Pro Player Stadium, Miami
XXXIV	2000	St. Louis Rams	Tennessee Titans	23-16	Georgia Dome, Atlanta
XXXVI	2001	Baltimore Ravens	New York Giants	34-7	Raymond James Stadium, Tampa
XXXVI	2002		New Orleans		Superdome, New Orleans
XXXVII	2003	New England Patriots	St. Louis Rams	20-17	Qualcomm Stadium, San Diego

* To get the year of the game (each January), add 1966 to the roman numeral listed in the left-most column
** All Super bowls were played in January or February, in the calendar year after the regular season

TABLE 4: SUPER BOWL GAMES

87

COLLEGE FOOTBALL SEASON

COLLEGE DIVISIONS AND CONFERENCES
Every Saturday, hundreds of college football teams face each other in competition. Just as the *NFL* is organized into *conferences* and *divisions*, so is college football. First, schools are divided by division — the top football schools are classified as Division I, the next best are Division II, and the smaller football programs are Division III. (Division I is further split into I-A and I-AA, with I-A containing the 112 most competitive schools.) The *NCAA* limits the number of football scholarships schools in each division may award, determining the number of talented players schools can attract.

Within each division, colleges are divided into regional conferences. There are also schools that do not belong to any conference, and they are called *independents*. There are 10 conferences in Division I-A. Below is a list of the 8 with the best football programs in the country:
- Atlantic Coast Conference (ACC)—9 schools in the Southeast
- Big Ten— 11 schools in the Midwest
- Big 12 — 12 schools in the Midwest and Texas
- Big East — 8 schools in the East
- Conference USA — 10 schools in the South and Midwest
- Pacific 10 (Pac-10) — 10 schools in the West
- Southeastern Conference (SEC) — 12 schools in the South
- Western Athletic Conference (WAC) —10 schools in the West and South

REGULAR SEASON
The college football *regular season* begins in early September and lasts through November or early December. Each team plays either 11 or 12 games, one against each team in its conference, and up to 4 games outside its conference. This is why most of college football's great rivalries are established within conferences. The team with the best record in games within its conference is declared the conference champion.

NATIONAL RANKINGS

Since some college teams play schedules against more difficult opponents than others, a better measure than just won-loss record is needed to rank them. Every week, two *polls* are taken that rank college teams #1 to #25. In one poll, the order is determined by a team of writers from the Associated Press (AP), and in the other, coaches rank the teams in the USA Today/ESPN poll. These rankings are often used to determine *bowl* match-ups (discussed below).

BOWL GAMES

In late December and early January, the top college teams play in over 20 *bowl games* across the country, with the best playing on or after New Year's Day. For each bowl, a committee invites teams to play in a large stadium, awarding the participating colleges millions of dollars by luring huge corporations to sponsor the event. Some bowls choose the top teams based on their national rankings. Other bowls invite teams from particular conferences each year. For example, the Rose Bowl historically has invited the champion of the Pac-10 and Big Ten Conferences to play there. Some of the major bowls are:

Orange Bowl — Miami, Fla.   Cotton Bowl — Dallas, Texas
Sugar Bowl — New Orleans, La.   Fiesta Bowl — Tempe, Arizona
Rose Bowl — Pasadena, Calif.   Citrus Bowl — Orlando, Fla.

THE BOWL CHAMPIONSHIP SERIES

College football has always relied on *polls* to determine the best team for the year. The *Bowl Championship Series* (BCS), started in 1998, aimed to make the system more objective by using a complex formula to determine the nation's 2 best teams that play for the National Championship. The BCS weighs 5 factors: 1) the average ranking of a team in the AP and USA Today/ESPN coaches' poll, 2) the average of 8 different computer rankings, 3) strength of schedule determined by win-loss records of opponents and opponents' opponents, 4) the number of losses by a team, and 5) "quality wins," or victories over Top 10-ranked teams. The 2 teams that score best then play to determine the *National Champion* at a site that rotates each year between the Fiesta, Sugar, Orange, and Rose bowls.

NFL COLLEGE DRAFT

Every year in late April, the *NFL Draft* is held at the Annual Player Selection Meeting in New York City. At the meeting, NFL teams choose which of the finest graduating college football players they want on their team. Some underclass players also choose to enter the draft. Teams select players one at a time in reverse order of the teams' *records* from the previous season, taking *playoff* results into account. For example, the team with the worst record selects first, the *Super Bowl Champion* selects last, the Super Bowl runner-up selects second-to-last, and so on. This system was established in 1935 to help the worst teams improve by allowing them to select the best of the young talent.

The draft has 7 *rounds*, meaning that each team has the opportunity to select 7 players, one per round. The first-round selection of the team that chooses first (the one with the worst record) is called the *first overall pick*. While each team tries to choose the most talented player still available when its turn comes, a team may need to place priority on filling a particular *position* where its *roster* is weak. Each draft pick can play only for the team that drafted him for his first 3 years in the league. After that, if his contract has expired, he becomes a *free agent*, which means he can entertain offers from other teams who would like his services.

Draft choices allotted to a team are its own property and may be traded at any point in the season to other teams for a current player or another *draft choice*. For example, the Colts might trade their first-round draft pick for the 49ers' second-round choice plus a 49er lineman. The 49ers would then have 2 first-round picks while the Colts would have 2 second-round picks.

Whenever *expansion teams* are added to the NFL, a separate *expansion draft* is held. Existing teams are permitted to protect a certain limited number of their key players, but have to leave most members of their team unprotected. The expansion teams then select from these players to create their rosters.

INTRODUCTION TO FANTASY LEAGUES

Imagine what it would be like to own a single team that combines the talents of the biggest *NFL* stars, like *Marshall Faulk*, *Randy Moss* and *Kurt Warner*. If this sounds like a fantasy you might enjoy, maybe you should try fantasy football, an enormously popular game played among friends who each "own" a team made up of between 10 and 25 *NFL* players. Whenever a player scores, he earns points for his fantasy team, so try to choose players who score often. Throughout the season, fantasy teams compete against each other on the basis of these points. When watching a game, you can always tell who is the fantasy football owner in a crowd, because he cares more about which player scores than which NFL team wins the game.

STARTING OUT: THE DRAFT
To select teams, fantasy owners meet before the season to take turns choosing NFL players in a process similar to the real NFL *Draft*. Some leagues and player drafts are run entirely over the Internet. Owners may draft only a certain number of players at each position, and each week during the season must choose which of these players are active and which "sit on the bench." Only active players may score points for their team.

EARNING POINTS
Fantasy players garner points for their owners in different ways, depending on how the league is set up. Most use basic offensive statistics such as *touchdowns*, *field goals*, *extra points* and yards gained. Often, the length of the touchdown or field goal determines its value.

COMPETITION
Most fantasy leagues are set up just like the NFL, where teams play a schedule of games against each other during the season. The team with the most points in each game wins, and towards the end of the season, the teams with the best records compete to determine the Fantasy Bowl champion. Other leagues merely keep a running tally of the points earned during a season, with the team having the most at the end of the year declared champion.

PRO FOOTBALL HALL OF FAME

The rich history of professional football is on display at the *Pro Football Hall of Fame* in Canton, Ohio, the birthplace of professional football. The Hall was first opened to the public in September 1963 as a 2-building complex. Two expansion projects in 1971 and 1978 added 2 more buildings, and a $9.1 million expansion project completed in 1995 added 64% more space in a fifth building that includes GameDay Stadium.

The Hall is filled with exhibition galleries, a large movie theater, a research library and a museum store, and each Hall of Fame member is honored separately in the Enshrinees Mementos Room. Most exhibits use electronics and video to encourage participation.

Members of the Hall of Fame are chosen by a 38-member Board of Selectors, consisting mostly of sports writers, including one from each *NFL* city (2 from New York). The board meets annually the day before the Super Bowl to elect a new class of inductees. Members can be players, coaches or other contributors (such as owners). Between 4 and 7 members are inducted each year, and to become a member, one needs to be named on 80% of the ballots cast by the Board. In addition, players are not eligible until they have been retired 5 years, although *coaches* can be elected as soon as they retire. In 2002, there were 216 members.

HALL OF FAME GAME
Since 1962, to kick off each *pre-season*, an NFL game is played in Canton in late July or early August, across the street from the Hall of Fame. The teams are chosen ahead of time and changed annually so that each team eventually gets a chance to participate.

NFL PRO BOWL

The *Pro Bowl* is an annual game between all-star teams from the *NFC* and *AFC*, held in Honolulu, Hawaii one week after the *Super Bowl*. It is an honor for a player to be selected to play.

AWARDS — COLLEGE & PRO

The following awards are given to honor players and coaches:

COLLEGE AWARDS

Heisman Trophy — Presented annually by the Downtown Athletic Club of New York to the best college football player in the country. Voting is done by national media and former Heisman winners.

All-America Team — A fictitious team consisting of the best college football players at each position, selected annually by the Associated Press (AP), Football Writers' Association, CNN/Sports Illustrated, The Sporting News, American Football Coaches' Association and the *Walter Camp* Foundation. A player selected to this team is called an *All-American*.

NFL AWARDS

Player of the Year / Most Valuable Player (*MVP*) — At least 5 separate organizations give their own MVP award to the player they consider to be the best in the *NFL*, including AP, Pro Football Weekly/Pro Football Writers' Association (PFW/PFWA), Sports Illustrated, The Sporting News, and Football Digest. Each year, the organizations usually select the same 1 or 2 players to receive their awards. AP also gives separate awards to both Defensive and Offensive Players of the Year.

Rookie of the Year — Awarded by these same organizations to the best first-year player; some give separate awards to Offensive and Defensive players.

AFC / NFC Coach of the Year — Awarded by USA Today to the best *head coach* in each *conference* and by several other groups to the NFL's best coach. Usually given to a coach whose team showed a large improvement over the previous year.

All-Pro / All-NFL Team — The AP and PFW/PFWA each select an All-Pro team, which is a fictitious team consisting of the best NFL players at each position. These lists are combined to form the All-NFL team.

PERSONALITIES – PAST & PRESENT

In this section you will find biographies of football's current stars and some of the most famous players of the past. Also included are coaches and other personalities you should become familiar with. Although there have been many great players over the years, limited space prevents us from listing them all here; please do not be disappointed if you do not find all your favorites. All statistics are current through the end of the 2001 season. The following key of abbreviations applies to this chapter:

A = active player
Hall = member of *Pro Football Hall of Fame*
TD = *touchdown*
QB = *quarterback*
RB = *running back*
WR = *wide receiver*
KR = *kick returner*

LB = *linebacker*
DB = *defensive back*
DL = *defensive lineman*
PK = *place kicker*
P = *punter*
MVP = *Most Valuable Player*
All-Pro = given annually to top players at each position

Baugh, Sammy: (QB, P, DB, Hall) This amazing all-around athlete was the first *quarterback* to make the *forward pass* a universally accepted part of football strategy. He was actually discovered on the minor-league baseball field where they dubbed him "Slingin' Sammy" for the way he could whip the ball around the field. Baugh went on to lead the NFL in passing a record 6 times between 1937 and 1949, helping the Washington Redskins win 2 *NFL Championships*. One year, he completed an unheard-of 70% of his passes! His amazing accomplishments at quarterback overshadowed incredible efforts as a *punter* and *defensive back*. Baugh still holds the NFL record for highest *punting average* in a career (45.1 yards) and in a season (an unbelievable 51.4 yards in 1940). When he concentrated on defense in 1943, he led the league with 11 *interceptions*. Baugh retired in 1953.

Blanda, George (QB, PK, Hall) No player in football history has been more durable or versatile than George Blanda. He started as a *place kicker* with the Chicago Bears in 1949 and went on to play 26 years as both a *quarterback* and kicker for the Bears, Baltimore Colts, Houston Oilers and Oakland Raiders. (The 2nd longest career was only 21 years.) He holds dozens of NFL records as both a kicker and passer — games played (340), *field goal attempts* (637) and passes *intercepted* (277) to name a few—and is 3rd all-time in career points (2,002). In 1961, he broke the single-season record for *TD passes* thrown with 36, a record not broken for 23 years (by *Dan Marino*). After age 40, Blanda had some of his best years as a kicker, scoring over 100 points in 3 straight seasons. In the 1970 season at age 43, he helped the Oakland Raiders either tie or win 5 games in a row with last-minute passing and kicking plays. Amazingly, Blanda played until age 48, retiring in 1975.

Bradshaw, Terry: (QB, Hall) Drafted in the *first round* by the perennial last-place *Pittsburgh Steelers* in 1970, this Louisiana Tech graduate was touted as the next great *quarterback* in the NFL because of his strong throwing arm and sturdy body. After struggling through 2 tough years where he threw over 40 *interceptions*, Bradshaw led the Steelers to an unprecedented 4 *Super Bowl* Championships in just 6 seasons (1974, 1975, 1978 and 1979) and was named *MVP* in the last 2. He was also NFL MVP in 1978. As a player, Bradshaw had the reputation of being simple, but he has proven to be a well-spoken studio analyst on CBS' "NFL Today" and Fox's "NFL Sunday" since 1990. Bradshaw has also appeared in several movies, TV episodes, and nutty commercials selling cheap long distance calls, has recorded three top-selling gospel albums and a Top-10 country hit, and even co-hosted the 2001 Country Music Awards.

Brown, Jim: (RB, Hall) His combination of brute strength and speed helped him become the all-time leading *rusher* in only 9 years. (His record of 12,312 yards has since been broken by 5 other players.) As an *All-American* out of Syracuse in 1957, Brown was *drafted* in the first *round* by the Cleveland Browns where he played 9 years without missing a single game. He was voted to the *Pro Bowl* each year and led the league in rushing every year but one. Brown still holds the all-time record for average yards per *rushing attempt* (5.2) and is fifth all-time in touchdowns (126). He retired in 1965 at age 30 while still in his prime and landed roles in action movies like "The Dirty Dozen." Brown, often seen wearing a colorful Muslim cap, is heavily active in African-American causes. He is founder and president of the Amer-I-Can program which teaches convicts and gang members life-management skills. Ironically, Brown has had his own share of legal problems having been charged several times with domestic violence since the 1960s and jailed in 2002 for refusing to pay a fine after smashing the windows of his wife's car.

Bryant, Bear: (Coach) Paul William "Bear" Bryant who grew up poor on a small Arkansas farm went on to become the winningest *coach* in college football history. He earned the nickname "Bear" early-on when he wrestled a bear on a theater stage for $5. After serving in the Navy for 4 years during World War II, Bryant developed a reputation as a demanding coach and strict disciplinarian in stints with the Universities of Maryland, Kentucky, and Texas A&M. But it was his 25 years prowling the sidelines in his signature houndstooth hat with the Alabama Crimson Tide that will forever be remembered. He led Alabama to 6 *national championships* and 24 *bowl games* during which time he was named National *Coach of the Year* 3 times. In his 38-year career, Bryant's teams won a then-Division I-A record 323 games (323-85-17), earned a place in 29 bowl games, and finished Top 10 in the polls 20 times. Sadly, Bryant died less than 2 months after retiring from coaching in 1982. So revered was he that in 1997 a U.S. postage stamp was designed to honor his memory. Not until 2001 did two coaches finally surpass or tie Bryant's record for wins – Joe Paterno (327) and Bobby Bowden (323).

Butkus, Dick: (LB, Hall) One of the most ferocious defensive players ever to play the game, Butkus was nicknamed "The Animal" and has even been accused of biting opponents. When asked who hit them the hardest, many old players name Butkus, who was even known to deck his own teammates in practice. His brutality must have had an effect, as he *recovered* 25 opponents' *fumbles* in his 9-year career, the 5th highest total ever. Chosen by the Chicago Bears in the first *round* of the 1965 *draft*, this *All-American* from the University of Illinois went on to make the *Pro Bowl* 7 straight times starting with his *rookie* year. A knee injury cut his career short, forcing him to retire in 1973.

Ditka, Mike: (Tight End, Coach, Hall) This intensely competitive former *coach* of the Chicago Bears started out as the team's fearless *tight end*. Drafted in the first *round* after an *All-American* career at the University of Pittsburgh, Ditka was one of the first tight ends in NFL history to combine excellent *receiving* and *blocking* skills. He won *Rookie of the Year* honors in 1961, catching passes for over 1,000 yards and 12 *TDs*, and was invited to the *Pro Bowl* in all 6 seasons with the Bears. Before retiring, he played 6 more years for the Philadelphia Eagles and *Dallas Cowboys*.

Ditka's legendary toughness on the field carried over to his coaching career. Often seen screaming at players on the sidelines during his 11 seasons as Bears' head *coach* (1982-1992), he compiled an impressive 112-68 record, led the team to its only *Super Bowl* victory (1986) and was named *Coach of the Year* twice (1986, 1988). Only a mild heart attack in 1988 mellowed him. When Ditka was fired after a dismal 1992 season, there was public outrage in Chicago over the treatment of this Bears' legend. In 1993, he began a career as studio analyst for the "NFL on NBC", but was lured back to coaching in 1997 for 3 gut-wrenching seasons with the New Orleans Saints where he averaged just 5 wins. Ditka retreated back to the studio in 2000, joining CBS' "NFL Today" pre-game show.

Elway, John: (QB) One of the steadiest *quarterbacks* in NFL history, Elway finally proved he could "win the big one" when the Denver Broncos won back-to-back *Super Bowls* in 1998 and 1999 after 3 Super Bowl defeats in the late 1980s. In the second Super Bowl victory, the final game of Elway's career, he won *MVP* honors with a 336-yard, two-TD performance. Elway was always a winner, having won more games as starting quarterback than any in NFL history and passing for more yards (51,475) than any quarterback besides *Dan Marino*. He was notorious for bringing his team back in the final moments of a game, engineering a record 47 fourth-quarter comebacks. The most memorable may have been a 15-play 98-yard series simply known as "The *Drive*" when Elway led Denver to a game-tying *touchdown* in the final moments of the 1986 *AFC* Championship game against the Cleveland Browns. Elway also won NFL MVP honors that year.

A remarkably durable athlete, Elway missed just 13 starts to injury in his 16-year NFL career. His throwing arm was so strong that the biggest complaint from receivers was how much their hands hurt when they caught the ball. An *All-American* in football at Stanford, Elway also played minor league baseball for the Yankees before being *drafted* as the NFL's *first overall pick* in 1983. He is an avid golfer and owns several automobile franchises in Colorado.

Faulk, Marshall: (RB, A) Combining power, speed and elusive moves, no NFL player today is a more potent all-around *offensive* threat. A three-time *All-American* at San Diego State, Faulk was the Indianapolis Colts' first-*round* pick in 1994, but it is with the St. Louis Rams who traded for him in 1999 that his talents truly emerged. Faulk excels at both *rushing* and *pass receiving* – he gained 2,429 total *yards from scrimmage* in 1999, the year he helped the Rams win the *Super Bowl*, and scored 26 TDs when he won the *MVP* award in 2000, both NFL single-season records. He is the only player ever to gain over 2,000 yards from scrimmage in 4 consecutive seasons. Marshall is an avid golfer during the off-season.

Favre, Brett: (QB, A) This kid from the backwoods of Mississippi has become the most durable and consistent quarterback in the NFL today. Favre is the only player ever to win 3 *MVP* awards (consecutive, 1995-97), during which time he led the *Green Bay Packers* to two straight *Super Bowls*, including a victory in Super Bowl XXXI. Despite injuries so painful that he became addicted to the painkiller Vicodin in the mid-1990s, Favre has not missed a single start in 10 years (157 games), an all-time record for a QB. During that stretch, he threw over 30 TD passes in 6 separate seasons, also a record. Favre is known for doing whatever it takes to win, whether it is tossing a two-yard shovel pass or rifling a perfectly placed *spiral* through heavy *coverage*. He is especially tough in Green Bay's icy Lambeau field, leading the Packers to a perfect 31-0 record when the temperature at game-time is 34 degrees or below. In 2001, the Packers signed Favre to a lifetime contract reportedly worth $100 million.

Grange, Harold (Red): (RB, Hall) Known as the "Galloping Ghost" for his gliding running style, Grange was integral to the introduction of professional football to Americans. His legend began at the University of Illinois, where he responded to important games with incredible performances. In a 1924 game against Michigan before 67,000 fans, the biggest crowd to ever see a game in the Midwest, Grange scored 4 *TD's* in the first 12 minutes, including a 95-yard *kickoff return* to begin the game. He added 2 *TD passes* and finished with an unheard-of 402 total yards. Grange capitalized on his stardom by becoming the first football player to make big money professionally, pocketing over $100,000 while playing for *George Halas'* Chicago Bears in 1925. Huge crowds packed arenas across the country to see this popular former college star, spurring an excitement over professional football that continues today.

Halas, George ("Pappa Bear"): (Coach, Hall) One of the NFL's founders, Halas also won more NFL games as a *coach* (324) than anyone else except *Don Shula*. Halas was one of the organizers of the *American Professional Football Association* in 1920 and actually suggested the name be changed to the *National Football League*. He bought the Chicago Bears in 1932 and coached them for 32 years before retiring in 1968. During his tenure, the Bears won 7 *NFL Championships*, including a 73-0 drubbing of the Washington Redskins in 1940. Halas helped establish many institutions of modern professional football. As coach, he was the first to hold daily practices and watch films to improve team performance. As owner, he pioneered the use of marching bands to entertain fans at *halftime*. Halas died in 1983 at age 88.

Harris, Franco: (RB, Hall) One of the most consistent *running backs* ever, Harris was the centerpiece of the relentless *Pittsburgh Steeler rushing* attack that helped the team win 4 *Super Bowls* in the 1970s. This *Hall of Famer* played in the NFL for 13 seasons and gained over 1,000 yards in 8 of them, finishing his career with 12,120 yards (8th all-time). He also rushed for more yards (354) in Super Bowls than any other player. Harris may best be remembered for the part he played in a 1972 *playoff* game against the Oakland Raiders. Trailing Oakland by a 7-6 score with 20 seconds remaining, Pittsburgh faced a desperate situation: fourth-and-10 from its own 40-yard line. On an attempted *passing play, quarterback Terry Bradshaw*'s pass ricocheted off of his *receiver*. However, the ball floated back towards the *line of scrimmage* right into Harris' hands, and he galloped 60 yards untouched for a game-winning TD, giving Pittsburgh its first playoff victory ever. This play will forever be known as the "immaculate reception."

Landry, Tom: (Coach, DB, Hall) Wearing his trademark fedora, he directed the *Dallas Cowboys* from the sidelines for 29 years, turning them from a terrible *expansion team* in 1960 into a consistent winner. This quiet and religious man led the Cowboys to 12 *division titles*, 7 *conference championships* and 2 *Super Bowl* victories (1972, 1978). His 20 *post-season* wins is the most by any NFL *coach*, and his 270 overall victories is 3rd-best all-time. After a dismal 1988 season saw the Cowboys win only 3 games, this coaching legend was fired by new owner Jerry Jones and replaced with University of Miami coach *Jimmy Johnson*, who then did what Landry had once done — rebuilt a losing team into a 2-time Super Bowl Champion. Landry was the *fullback* for the University of Texas when it won the *Sugar Bowl* in 1947 and the *Orange Bowl* in 1949. He became an *All-Pro cornerback* with the New York Giants, playing from 1950-1955 before getting into coaching.

Lombardi, Vince: (Coach, Hall) One of football's greatest legends, Lombardi coached the *Green Bay Packers* to an incredible 5 *NFL Championships* in only 7 seasons (1961-1967), including victories in *Super Bowls* I and II. His overall *winning percentage* of .740 (105-35-6) is the highest of any *coach* with over 100 wins. Rather than use fancy plays and complex strategies, Lombardi was an advocate of simple hard-nosed football, striving for the perfect execution of a small variety of *running plays* and short passes. He became terminally ill soon after coaching the Washington Redskins in 1969 and died in 1970. To honor him, the NFL's *Lombardi Trophy* is awarded each year to the team that wins the Super Bowl. He coined the now-immortal phrase "winning is not everything — it's the only thing."

99

Madden, John (Coach, Commentator) This animated former NFL head *coach* is the most popular football commentator on television. Over the past 22 years as an analyst at CBS and Fox, Madden pioneered the use of tools to help TV viewers understand football. Using the "CBS Chalkboard", Madden drew lines on top of *instant replay* images to help the viewer see the intricacies of a play, a technique imitated by other sports telecasts. A top commercial spokesman, he has won 13 Emmy Awards for broadcasting and written four best-selling books on football. "Madden NFL" by EA Sports is the best-selling sports video game ever.

Madden started as an extremely successful head coach of the Oakland Raiders from 1969-78, leading them to the playoffs 7 out of 10 years and a victory in *Super Bowl* XI. He compiled the best regular-season *winning percentage* in history, victorious 75% of the time. Despite his success, the daily stress of coaching gave the portly Madden stomach ulcers, forcing him to switch in 1980 to coaching spectators from the CBS broadcast booth. In 1994, Madden left CBS for the Fox Network where he earned $7.5 million per year for 8 seasons. In 2002 he joined ABC's *Monday Night Football*. Even with a hectic schedule, Madden still refuses to fly on airplanes, often traveling thousands of miles by bus to get to games.

Marino, Dan: (QB) *Drafted* in the *first round* by the *Miami Dolphins* in 1983, this University of Pittsburgh *quarterback* with the lightning-quick release quickly became the most prolific *passer* in NFL history, setting dozens of records. After winning *Rookie of the Year* honors in 1983, in only his second season he shattered all-time marks by throwing for 5,084 yards and 48 *TDs* (the previous best had been only 36 TDs by *George Blanda*). His durability was equally as impressive — he passed for over 3,000 yards the next 8 seasons in a row. When he retired after the 1999 season, Marino had amassed a staggering 420 TD passes and 61,361 yards passing, literally miles ahead of any other player. Despite all his accomplishments, no team Marino played on ever won a championship, even when he was a kid. Marino loves to be the center of attention, ready with a story for any occasion. Dan and wife Claire established the Dan Marino Foundation in 1992 to help children with disabilities, a cause especially poignant to the Marinos as one of their 5 children is autistic.

Montana, Joe: (QB, Hall) Drafted out of Notre Dame in 1979 as only a third-*round* choice by the *San Francisco 49ers* (the 82nd player chosen overall), Montana went on to lead the team to 4 *Super Bowl* victories in 4 appearances during the 1980s (1982, 1985, 1989 and 1990). Considered by many to be the best big-game *quarterback* of all-time, Montana was named *MVP* in 3 of those Super Bowls, setting records for most *TD passes* in a Super Bowl (5 against Denver in 1990) and most passing yards (357 against Cincinnati in 1989). No quarterback has totaled more career TDs or passing yards in Super Bowls than Montana. For engineering 31 fourth-quarter comebacks in his career, he was dubbed "The Comeback Kid." Joe was also twice-named league MVP (1989, 1990). Montana's uncanny ability to throw accurate short passes while running at full speed fit perfectly with an offensive style pioneered by then-49er coach *Bill Walsh* that relied on short passes to move the ball down the field. Playing in this system for 14 years helped Montana complete 63% of his passes over his career, the third-best percentage ever, and throw 273 TD passes, 7th best all-time.

Despite suffering a series of career-threatening injuries to his back and throwing elbow, Montana was still considered a top NFL quarterback at age 38. Unable to play for nearly 2 full seasons after surgery for severe elbow tendonitis, the 49ers, in an unpopular move, traded him to the Kansas City Chiefs in 1993. Healthy once again, he promptly led the Chiefs to their first *conference championship* game in 24 years. In 1996, after 16 years in the NFL, Montana retired. Montana's nationwide popularity landed him endorsement deals worth more than $5 million per year. So revered was he that a town in the state of Montana changed its name to Joe, Montana.

Moss, Randy: (WR, A) One of the NFL's most feared *receivers*, Moss is criticized for his negative attitude nearly as often as he is praised for his amazing talents. Moss' world-class speed and leaping ability helped him set several conference records in just two years at Marshall University, including a then-*Division* I-record 25 TD catches in 1997. However, a couple of arrests and even a stint in jail influenced several NFL teams to pass him over in the *draft* before the Minnesota Vikings chose him 21st. Their gamble paid off as Moss earned NFL *Rookie of the Year* honors in 1998 and became the only player ever to gain 1,000 yards each of his first four seasons. Moss has shown a remarkable ability to catch long TD passes, scoring 53 TDs in just 64 games, 34 of them over 40 yards. Although he has steered clear of the law since joining the NFL, after signing a $75 million contract extension in 2001, he was criticized by his teammates for whining and not playing hard, even quoted as saying that he only plays "when I want to play."

Namath, Joe: (QB, Hall) Known as "Broadway Joe" for the glamorous lifestyle he led, Namath is best remembered for guaranteeing a victory in *Super Bowl* III and delivering on his promise. The 16-7 win by his New York Jets over the heavily-favored Baltimore Colts established the *AFL's* credibility as a worthy counterpart to the NFL. Namath started his college career under *Bear Bryant* at the University of Alabama who called him "the greatest athlete" he had ever coached. After being named *MVP* of the 1965 *Orange Bowl,* Namath was lured to the Jets with a $400,000 signing bonus, an amount never before given to a professional athlete. Namath quickly demonstrated his worth by earning *Rookie of the Year* honors in 1965. In 1967, he became the first player to *pass* for over 4,000 yards in a season, a feat not repeated for 12 years. In addition to possessing a great throwing arm that could heave perfect *spirals,* Namath was strong and agile until 4 major knee surgeries slowed him down, eventually forcing him to retire in 1977. Since then, Joe has acted in several dramatic plays, appeared in a TV movie and series, and represented several companies as a spokesperson, including Classic Sports Network and CBS Sportsline.

Payton, Walter: (RB, Hall) Called "Sweetness" by his teammates, in his 13 seasons with the Chicago Bears, Payton *rushed* for more yards (16,726) than any other player in NFL history. This first-*round draft choice* out of Jackson State in 1975 ran for over 100 yards in a game a record 77 times. In 1977, Payton won the league's *MVP* award and broke *O.J. Simpson*'s record by gaining an incredible 275 yards on the ground in one game! Although soft-spoken in private, Payton was a very tough player on the field, choosing to butt heads with a defender if it meant getting a couple of extra yards at the end of a run. In 1998 he established the Walter Payton Foundation to help neglected and abused children in Illinois. He also liked to drive race cars and was co-owner of an Indy car racing team. Tragically, Sweetness died of liver cancer in 1999 at the age of 45. In honor of his outstanding college career, the Walter Payton Award is given each year to the nation's oustanding Division I-AA football player.

Rice, Jerry (WR, A) Considered by most to be the best pass *receiver* of all time, Rice holds nearly every receiving record in the books. He already has scored more *TDs* in his brilliant 17-year career with the *San Francisco 49ers* and Oakland Raiders than any other player (196), including the most *TD passes* in a single season in 1987, when he caught 22 and was named league *MVP*. The following year Rice was named MVP of *Super Bowl* XXIII with an incredible 11-catch, 215-yard performance. He has also gained at least 1,000 yards receiving in 13 seasons and has more career receiving yards (20,386) than any other player by far.

Chosen as the 49ers' first-*round draft choice* in 1985 out of Division I-AA Mississippi Valley State, Rice has reaped the benefits of playing with great *quarterbacks* for nearly his entire career — *Joe Montana* for his first 6 years, and *Steve Young* in the next 9. Despite early criticism that he had only average speed for a wide receiver, Rice became a superstar by combining elusive moves with the ability to catch almost any ball thrown his way. He is known for his strict work ethic, training intensely during the off-season and arriving to training camp long before the other *veterans*. Rice's conditioning helped him play his first 12 NFL seasons without missing a single game to injury. This 188-game streak was broken in 1997 when he tore ligaments in his left knee, but following surgery he started a new streak in 1998 and hasn't missed a game since. A 49er legend, Rice was released by the team in 2001 to make room for younger players. He was signed by the Raiders across the Bay, where at age 39, he pulled off yet another 1,000-yard season.

Rozelle, Pete: (*Commissioner,* Hall) Recognized as the greatest sports commissioner ever, Alvin "Pete" Rozelle is credited with growing the *NFL* into the wildly popular spectator sport that it is today. A surprise selection to the job in 1960 at the age of 33, Rozelle presided over the NFL for nearly 3 decades during its growth from 12 to 28 teams. He changed Sundays forever when he negotiated the first league-wide TV contract with CBS in 1962 and also sold the idea for *Monday Night Football* to ABC in 1969 where it is still the longest-running sports series today. Rozelle also negotiated the NFL-*AFL* merger that led to the first *Super Bowl* in 1967, and he landed the NFL its first huge TV contract in 1982, a $2.1 billion deal with 3 networks. He had such an impact on the game that he was elected to the *Pro Football Hall of Fame* in 1985 while still Commissioner, an honor usually given only to those who are retired. Rozelle did retire in 1989 and in 1996 died from brain cancer at the age of 70. In 1999 he was named the most powerful person in sports in the 20th Century by The Sporting News.

Sanders, Barry: (RB) One of the most electrifying runners in NFL history, Sanders' sharp changes of direction often left would-be *tacklers* grasping at only air. At 5' 8", his low-to-the-ground running style helped him gain 15,269 yards in his brilliant 10-year NFL career, third-most ever. Before his NFL success, Sanders set 13 NCAA records at Oklahoma State, including a record 2,628 yards rushing in his *Heisman Trophy*-winning junior year. As a *rookie* chosen by the Detroit Lions in the first *round* of the 1989 *draft,* Sanders broke team records for rushing yards and *touchdowns* and won NFL *Rookie of the Year* honors. In a spectacular 1997 season,

Sanders won the NFL's *MVP* award by *rushing* for 2,053 yards, the second-best total ever, and his 4th NFL rushing title. His 10 consecutive seasons rushing for 1,000 yards has been surpassed only by *Emmitt Smith*. Over his career, Barry averaged an incredible 5.0 yards per carry. The humble Sanders attributed all of his success to his *offensive line* and God (in that order). Surprisingly, Barry decided to retire in 1999 at age 31 with no explanation.

Sayers, Gale (RB, KR, Hall) In his relatively short career, Sayers impressed more observers with his running ability than any other player. He had the magical ability to stop on a dime, change directions and accelerate out of sight with a burst of speed (he ran the 100-yard dash in just 9.5 seconds). A 2-time *All-American* from the University of Kansas, he was *drafted* in 1965 by the Chicago Bears in the *first round*. He set a *rookie* record by scoring 22 *TDs* (6 in one game), earning him *Rookie of the Year* honors along with teammate *Dick Butkus*. Sayers was also an explosive *kickoff returner* who still holds the all-time record for highest *return average* (30.6 yards). In 1968, at the peak of his career, a severe knee injury sent him to the operating table. Through perseverance and the help of his friend Brian Piccolo, Sayers recovered to lead the NFL in *rushing* the very next season. When Sayers accepted the *George Halas* Award in 1970 for being the league's most courageous player, he dedicated it to Piccolo who was dying from cancer. Their relationship was the subject of the 1971 hit TV movie "Brian's Song" which was re-made in 2001.

Shula, Don: (Coach, Hall) Shula's record as *head coach* of the Baltimore Colts (1963-1969) and the *Miami Dolphins* (1970-1995) is unmatched. This strict disciplinarian retired in 1996 as the winningest coach in NFL history (347-173-6, .665). In 33 seasons, his teams finished below .500 only twice and appeared in a record 6 *Super Bowls* (2 wins).

When the Dolphins lured Shula away from the Colts in 1970 after he helped them win 2 *division* titles and the 1968 *NFL Championship*, Commissioner *Pete Rozelle*, in a controversial move, awarded the Dolphins' #1 *draft choice* to the Colts as compensation, claiming Shula had been recruited without the Colts' permission. He went on to lead Miami to 10 *divisional titles*, 5 *AFC Championships* and 2 consecutive Super Bowl victories (1973, 1974). Super Bowl VII was the culmination of the only undefeated season in NFL history (1972-73), as the Dolphins went 14-0 during the season and 3-0 in the playoffs. Coaching runs in the Shula family, as Don's son David was the Cincinnati Bengals' head coach from 1992-96 and his son Mike is the *quarterback* coach for the Dolphins. Don is such a legend in Miami that a freeway is named after him.

Simpson, O.J. (Orenthal James): (RB, Hall) Regarded as one of the most talented runners of all-time, the man many call "The Juice" will be forever remembered as an accused double-murderer who was aquitted in a criminal trial only to be found civilly liable for the deaths of his ex-wife and her friend to the tune of $33.5 million. Born in the ghettos of San Francisco in 1947, O.J. overcame rickets to become a star running back at the University of Southern California, winning the *Heisman Trophy* in 1968. He was chosen as the first player in the 1968 *draft* by the Buffalo Bills, where he shattered numerous *rushing* records from 1968-1977. O.J. was the first player ever to run for over 2,000 yards in a season (2,003 in only 14 games in 1973), breaking *Jim Brown*'s record that stood for 10 years. That season, Simpson gained over 200 yards rushing in a game 3 times, averaged an incredible 6.0 yards per carry, and was voted NFL *MVP*.

Simpson wrapped up his career with the *San Francisco 49ers* in 1979 after several knee injuries had slowed him down. Despite finishing his career with 11,236 yards (11th-best all-time) and being inducted into the *Hall of Fame*, his teams never won a single playoff game. After retirement, Simpson's dynamic personality and good looks landed him a job as one of the first African-American celebrity pitchmen, endorsing Hertz rental cars in ads where he ran through airports, leaping over obstacles to reach his flight. He also took acting roles in several films and worked as the studio football analyst for NBC sports in the 1980s and 1990s.

Smith, Emmitt: (RB, A) Known simply as "Emmitt", he is one of the best *running backs* of all-time, having rushed for a record 148 TDs and 16,187 yards, second only to *Walter Payton* who he is likely to pass in 2002. In 1993, 1994 and 1996, he helped his *Dallas Cowboys* win *Super Bowl* championships, and in 1995 he set an all-time record for rushing TDs in a season with 25. In his spectacular 12-year career, he has rushed for 1,000 yards a record 11 times. At only 5' 9", he is the prototypical stocky running back, difficult for *tacklers* to grab because he is so low to the ground. Emmitt was a first-*round draft pick* out of the University of Florida in 1990 where he was an *All-American*. He keeps the footballs from every touchdown he has scored in both college and the NFL.

Tarkenton, Fran: (QB, Hall) Before *Dan Marino* passed him in 1995, Tarkenton had thrown for more yards (47,003) and *TDs* (342) than any other *quarterback* in the history of the NFL, probably because he lasted so long — 18 years. He was known as an intelligent quarterback with the ability to *scramble* away from defenders. Despite this ability, he was *sacked* more times (483) than any other QB except *John Elway* and Dave Krieg. This son of a Methodist minister was *drafted* by the Minnesota Vikings in 1961 out of the University of Georgia and played for them in two separate stints. In the '70s, he led the Vikings to 6 straight NFC Central *division titles* and 3 *Super Bowls* in 4 years. Unfortunately, his team lost all 3, leading to criticism that he could not win "the big one." Since retirement, Tarkenton has become a prolific entrepreneur, starting or running 12 businesses including several computer-related firms. He is also a motivational speaker who teaches audiences how to overcome setbacks, and author of the aptly named book "What Losing Taught Me About Winning." Tarkenton is also well known for having hosted the hit TV show "That's Incredible".

Unitas, Johnny: (QB, Hall) Nicknamed "The Ice Man" by admirers of his coolness under pressure, Unitas had set every passing record in the books by the end of the 1960s. All this coming from a man that was cut by the *Pittsburgh Steelers* after they *drafted* him in 1955. The Baltimore Colts picked Unitas up the next year, and in the 1958 *NFL Championship* game, he assured his place in football history by leading the Colts to a comeback victory in *overtime* against the New York Giants by manufacturing two 80-yard scoring *drives*. This was the first of 4 NFL Championships he won with the Colts, including one *Super Bowl*. In his 17 years with the team, Unitas was named *All-Pro* 6 times and won the *MVP* award 3 times. Many of his records have been broken, but one record that may never fall is his streak of 47 consecutive games in which he threw at least one *TD pass*.

Warner, Kurt: (QB, A) The ultimate Cinderella story, Warner went from supermarket stock-boy to *Super Bowl MVP* in just five years. Cut by the *Green Bay Packers* in 1994, he worked his way up through the *Arena Football League* (1995-97) and *NFL Europe* (1998). When St. Louis Rams' starting QB Trent Green hurt his knee during the 1999 *pre-season*, at age 28 Warner became the starter and led the Rams to a 13-3 record and its first-ever Super Bowl victory, earning himself MVP of both the season and Super Bowl. That year, he threw for an amazing 41 TDs (3rd-best season ever) and a Super Bowl record 414 yards, including a 73-yard TD pass with under 2 minutes left that won the game. Warner continues to astound, passing for 4,830 yards (2nd-best ever) and winning another MVP in 2001 while taking the Rams to another Super Bowl. He is now recognized as the NFL's top QB, leading the potent Rams' *offense* to an unprecedented 3 straight 500-point seasons and becoming the highest-rated (103.0) and most accurate (66.9% *completion percentage*) passer in NFL history. Known as a deeply religious and kind-hearted man, Warner adoped his wife's two children from a previous marriage, one of whom is blind and mentally disabled from a childhood accident, before they had two of their own.

White, Reggie: (DL) Probably the most dominant *defensive lineman* of the '80s and '90s, this 4-time *All-Pro* is the all-time leader in *sacks* (198) despite often being *double-* and *triple-teamed* by opponents. *Drafted* out of the *USFL* by the Philadelphia Eagles in 1984, this 6'5", 300-pounder from the University of Tennessee was gifted with incredible strength and good speed. White hit the jackpot in 1993 when he signed a 4-year $17 million contract with the *Green Bay Packers*, making him the richest lineman in NFL history. He then helped lead the team to 2 straight *Super Bowl* appearances (1997, 1998), including a victory in Super Bowl XXXI. White retired in 1999 due to persistent back problems, only to return for one final season with the Carolina Panthers in 2000. His fans call him the "Minister of Defense", as he is an ordained Baptist minister.

Young, Steve: (QB) After spending 4 seasons on the bench as *Joe Montana's backup*, Young emerged as the premier *quarterback* in the NFL. His road to success was more than a little bumpy, though. When he graduated from Brigham Young University in 1984 (he is the great-great-great grandson of Brigham Young), instead of joining the NFL, Young signed a lucrative deal with the Los Angeles Express of the start-up *United States Football League* (*USFL*). However, when that league ran into financial difficulties after 2 years, he got out of his contract and joined the NFL's Tampa Bay Buccaneers. Young floundered as that team won only 4 games in 2 years. With his value at an all-time low, he was traded to the *San Francisco 49ers* in 1987 to become Montana's replacement in case of injury. It was not until Montana's throwing elbow required surgery in 1991 that Young was given a chance.

He made the most of this golden opportunity. Young became the then-most accurate passer in NFL history with a *passer's rating* of 96.8, leading the NFL in passing 6 of his first 7 years as the starter, while compiling a passer's rating that surpassed 100 in 5 of those (his 112.8 in 1994 is an NFL record). Voted league *MVP* twice (1992, 1994), so brilliant was his play that when Montana came back from injury in 1993, Young kept the starting job and Joe was traded. Despite his accomplishments, 49er fans still criticized him for not winning the big games. In 1995 he silenced them by leading the team to a *Super Bowl* victory with his NFL record 6 *TD passes*. Repeated concussions forced Young to retire in 2000 after 15 seasons. Currently a studio analyst for ESPN's "NFL Countdown", Young also is very active in children's charities, including the Forever Young Foundation which he founded. Young holds a law degree from BYU.

GREAT TEAMS & DYNASTIES

Green Bay Packers 1960-1967 — (72-24-4, 9-1 post-season)
Led by coaching legend *Vince Lombardi*, this team won 5 *NFL Championships* in only 7 years, including *Super Bowls* I and II. The Packers' offense heavily favored the run, scoring an NFL record 36 *rushing TDs* in 1962, led by its *fullback* Jim Taylor and *halfback* Paul Hornung. They also had one of the most accurate *QBs* ever in Bart Starr, who once threw 294 passes in a row without an *interception*.

Miami Dolphins 1971-1974 — (47-8-1, 8-2 post-season)
The Dolphins won back-to-back *Super Bowls* (VII and VIII), the first capping the only undefeated season in NFL history (17-0). Coach *Don Shula* relied on a running game led by bruising *fullback* Larry Csonka and *halfbacks* Mercury Morris and Jim Kiick, while QB Bob Griese (pronounced Greasy) threw to *WR* Paul Warfield.

Pittsburgh Steelers 1974-1979 — (67-20-1, 13-2 post-season)
This team rose from a history of losing to become the first team to win 4 *Super Bowls* (IX, X, XIII and XIV). Its awesome "Steel Curtain" defense, led by Mean Joe Greene, Jack Ham, Jack Lambert and Mel Blount, helped the Steelers dominate the *AFC's Central Division* 6 years in a row. The offense relied on *Franco Harris'* rushing and QB *Terry Bradshaw's* throwing to WRs Lynn Swann and John Stallworth.

San Francisco 49ers 1981-1990 — (112-39-1, 14-5 post-season)
In a 10-year span, this team won 4 *Super Bowls* (XVI, XIX, XXIII and XXIV) and finished at the top of the *NFC Western Division* 8 times. The 49ers were led by 2-time *MVP QB Joe Montana* and a potent offense designed by *Bill Walsh*, which relied on running plays and short passes. Montana's favorite targets were the amazing *Jerry Rice*, John Taylor, Dwight Clark and *RB* Roger Craig.

Dallas Cowboys 1992-1996 — (49-15, 10-1 post-season)
The Cowboys went from winning only 1 game in 1989 to winning 3 *Super Bowls* in 1993, 1994 and 1996. The team used high *draft picks* to choose QB Troy Aikman and *RB Emmitt Smith*, and hired coach *Jimmy Johnson* to replace the legendary *Tom Landry*. After Johnson quit in 1994, new coach Barry Switzer led the team to its 3rd Super Bowl victory in 4 years in spite of what many considered to be poor coaching on his part.

NFL INDIVIDUAL RECORDS
(Regular season only — Current through 2001 season)

Key: TD = Touchdown, FG = Field Goal, PAT = Point-After-Touchdown
* = Active Player

CAREER LEADERS

All-Time Passing Yards

Player	Team	Years	Passing Yards
Dan Marino	Miami	17	61,361
John Elway	Baltimore, Denver	16	51,475
Warren Moon	Houston, Minnesota, Seattle	17	49,325
Fran Tarkenton	Minnesota, NY Giants	18	47,003
Dan Fouts	San Diego	15	43,040
Joe Montana	San Francisco, Kansas City	15	40,551
Johnny Unitas	Baltimore, San Diego	18	40,239
Brett Favre*	Green Bay	11	38,627
Dave Krieg	Sea, KC, Det, Ariz, Chi, Hou	19	38,147
Boomer Esiason	Cincinnati, NY Jets, Arizona	14	37,920

All-Time Touchdown Passes

Player	Team	Years	TD Passes
Dan Marino	Miami	17	420
Fran Tarkenton	Minnesota, NY Giants	18	342
John Elway	Baltimore, Denver	16	300
Warren Moon	Houston, Minnesota, Seattle	17	291
Johnny Unitas	Baltimore, San Diego	18	290

All-Time Rushing Yards

Player	Team	Years	Rushing Yards
Walter Payton	Chicago	13	16,726
Emmitt Smith*	Dallas	12	16,187
Barry Sanders	Detroit	10	15,269
Eric Dickerson	LA Rams, Indianapolis, LA Raiders, Atlanta	11	13,259
Tony Dorsett	Dallas	12	12,739
Jim Brown	Cleveland	9	12,312
Marcus Allen	LA Raiders, Kansas City	16	12,243
Franco Harris	Pittsburgh	13	12,120
Thurman Thomas	Buffalo	13	12,074
John Riggins	NY Jets, Washington	14	11,352

109

All-Time Rushing Touchdowns

Player	Team	Years	Rushing TDs
Emmitt Smith*	Dallas	12	148
Marcus Allen	LA Raiders, Kansas City	16	123
Walter Payton	Chicago	13	110
Jim Brown	Cleveland	9	106
John Riggins	NY Jets, Washington	14	104

All-Time Receiving Yards

Player	Team	Years	Receiving Yards
Jerry Rice*	San Francisco, Oakland	17	20,386
James Lofton	Green Bay, LA Raiders, Buffalo, Philly	16	14,004
Cris Carter	Philadelphia, Minnesota	15	13,833
Henry Ellard	LA Rams, Washington	16	13,777
Tim Brown*	LA Raiders, Oakland	14	13,237
Andre Reed	Buffalo	16	13,198
Steve Largent	Seattle	14	13,089
Irving Fryar	New England, Miami, Philly	17	12,785
Art Monk	Washington	16	12,721
Charlie Joiner	Houston, Cincinnati, San Diego	18	12,146

All-Time Receiving Touchdowns

Player	Team	Years	Receiving TDs
Jerry Rice*	San Francisco, Oakland	17	185
Cris Carter	Philadelphia, Minnesota	15	129
Steve Largent	Seattle	14	100
Don Hutson	Green Bay	11	99
Tim Brown*	LA Raiders, Oakland	14	95

All-Time Total Touchdowns

Player	Team	Years	Total TDs
Jerry Rice*	San Francisco, Oakland	17	196
Emmitt Smith*	Dallas	12	159
Marcus Allen	LA Raiders, Kansas City	16	145
Cris Carter	Philadelphia, Minnesota	15	130
Jim Brown	Cleveland	9	126
Walter Payton	Chicago	13	125

All-Time Total Points

Player	Team	Years	TDs	FGs	PATs	Points
Gary Anderson*	Pittsburgh, Philly, SF, Minn.	20	0	476	705	2,133
Morten Andersen*	New Orleans, Atlanta, NYG	20	0	464	644	2,036
George Blanda	Chicago,Balt.,Hou.,Oakland	26	9	335	943	2,002
Norm Johnson	Seattle, Atl., Pitt., Philly	18	0	366	638	1,736
Nick Lowery	New England, KC, NY Jets	18	0	383	562	1,711

All-Time Sacks (record kept since 1982)

Player	Team	Years	Sacks
Reggie White	Philadelphia, Green Bay	15	198
Bruce Smith*	Buffalo, Washington	17	186
Kevin Greene	St. Louis, Pitt., Carolina, SF	15	160
Chris Doleman	Minnesota, Atlanta, SF	14	150 ½
Richard Dent	Chicago, Indy, Philly	15	137 ½

SINGLE-SEASON RECORDS

Single-Season Passing Yards

Player	Team	Season	Passing Yards
Dan Marino	Miami	1984	5,084
Kurt Warner*	St. Louis	2001	4,830
Dan Fouts	San Diego	1981	4,802
Dan Marino	Miami	1986	4,746
Dan Fouts	San Diego	1980	4,715

Single-Season Touchdown Passes

Player	Team	Season	TD Passes
Dan Marino	Miami	1984	48
Dan Marino	Miami	1986	44
Kurt Warner*	St. Louis	1999	41
Brett Favre*	Green Bay	1996	39
Brett Favre*	Green Bay	1995	38

Single-Season Rushing Yards

Player	Team	Season	Rushing Yards
Eric Dickerson	LA Rams	1984	2,105
Barry Sanders	Detroit	1997	2,053
Terrell Davis*	Denver	1998	2,008
O.J. Simpson	Buffalo	1973	2,003
Earl Campbell	Houston	1980	1,934

Single-Season Rushing Touchdowns

Player	Team	Season	Rushing TDs
Emmitt Smith*	Dallas	1995	25
John Riggins	Washington	1983	24
Joe Morris	NY Giants	1985	21
Emmitt Smith*	Dallas	1994	21
Terry Allen*	Washington	1996	21
Terrell Davis*	Denver	1998	21

Single-Season Receiving Yards

Player	Team	Season	Receiving Yards
Jerry Rice*	San Francisco	1995	1,848
Isaac Bruce*	St. Louis	1995	1,781
Charley Hennigan	Houston	1961	1,746
Herman Moore*	Detroit	1995	1,686
Marvin Harrison*	Indianapolis	1999	1,663

Single-Season Receiving Touchdown

Player	Team	Season	Receiving TDs
Jerry Rice*	San Francisco	1987	22
Mark Clayton	Miami	1984	18
Sterling Sharpe	Green Bay	1994	18
7 Players Tied			17

Single-Season Sacks (record kept since 1982)

Player	Team	Season	Sacks
Michael Strahan*	NY Giants	2001	22 ½
Mark Gastineau	NY Jets	1984	22
Reggie White	Philadelphia	1987	21
Chris Doleman	Minnesota	1989	21
Lawrence Taylor	NY Giants	1986	20 ½

SINGLE-GAME RECORDS

Best Passing Performances

Player	Team	Date	Passing Yards
Norm Van Brocklin	LA Rams	Sep 28, 1951	554
Warren Moon	Houston	Dec 16, 1990	527
Boomer Esiason	Arizona	Nov 10, 1996	522

Best Rushing Performances

Player	Team	Date	Rushing Yards
Corey Dillon*	Cincinnati	Oct 22, 2000	278
Walter Payton	Chicago	Nov 20, 1977	275
O.J. Simpson	Buffalo	Nov 25, 1976	273

Best Receiving Performances

Player	Team	Date	Receiving Yards
Flipper Anderson	LA Rams	Nov 26, 1989	336
Stephone Paige	Kansas City	Dec 22, 1985	309
Jim Benton	Cleveland	Nov 22, 1945	303

GLOSSARY

American Bowl: an annual *NFL pre-season* game played at an international site to expose citizens of other countries to the excitement of American football.

Arena Football League: founded in 1987, this popular indoor professional football league plays games on a small field 50 yards long by 85 feet wide, with 8 players per team; its 16 teams play in the spring and summer, during the *NFL's* off-season; *touchdowns, field goals,* and *safeties* are worth the same number of points as in NFL or *NCAA* football games, though Arena games generally have more *passing* and scoring.

Astroturf: an artificial surface used instead of grass on many football *fields.*

audible: verbal commands shouted by the *quarterback* to his teammates at the *line of scrimmage* to change a play on short notice.

backfield: the area behind the *line of scrimmage.*

backs: the *running backs;* the *halfback* and the *fullback.*

ball carrier: any player who has *possession* of the ball.

BCS (Bowl Championship Series): a complex and controversial ranking system established in 1998 which grants the 2 top-ranked college teams the right to play for the National Championship; weighs several factors including polls, computer rankings and team win-loss records.

beat: when a player gets past an opponent trying to *block* or *tackle* him.

blackout: when a regional network TV affiliate is forbidden from showing a local game because it is not sold out.

blitz: a play where the defensive team sends players *rushing* towards the *line of scrimmage* as soon as the ball is *snapped* to try to *sack* the *quarterback.*

blocking: the act of preventing a defensive player from getting to the *ball carrier; blockers* use their arms and bodies but may not *hold* an opponent.

bomb: a long *pass* thrown to a *receiver* sprinting down the field.

bowl game: a college football game played in late December or early January, after the regular season, between two successful teams.

bump-and-run: a technique used by *pass defenders,* where they hit a *receiver* once within 5 yards (1 yard in college) of the *line of scrimmage* to slow him down, and then follow him to prevent him from catching a pass.

bye: an automatic pass to the next playoff round given to a team.

call a play: instruct players to execute a pre-planned play.

clipping: *blocking* an opponent from behind below the waist; this illegal block is a *personal foul,* punishable by a 15-yard *penalty.* **113** complete pass: a *forward pass* to a teammate who catches it before it hits the ground.

conferences: groups into which teams are divided in professional and college football; the *NFL* is divided into *National* and *American* Conferences.

controlling the game clock: the use of tactics by an offensive team to either save or use up time on the *game clock*; often dictates its choice of plays.

cover or coverage: preventing a player from gaining yards; in *pass coverage*, a defender follows a *receiver* to prevent him from catching a pass; in *kick coverage*, members of the *kicking team* try to prevent a long kick *return*.

cut back: a sudden change in direction taken by a *ball carrier* to make it more difficult for defenders to follow and *tackle* him.

dead ball: a ball becomes dead when a play is over and becomes *live* as soon as it is *snapped* for the next play.

division: in the *NFL*, sub-groups within conferences, such as the *Eastern, Northern, Southern* and *Western Divisions*; also, a grouping of teams in college football, where Division I contains the most competitive teams and Division III the least.

double coverage or double team: when 2 defensive players *cover* one *receiver*, or when 2 offensive players *block* one defender.

down: one of 4 chances a team on offense has to gain 10 yards; also, the state of a player who has just been *tackled*; also, a ball that a player touches to the ground in the *end zone* to get a *touchback* or a punted ball touched first by a player on the kicking team, which is considered dead where it was touched.

down the field: in the direction of the opponent's *goal line*.

draft choice or pick: a player chosen by a professional sports team from a pool of eligible players.

drive: the series of plays a team puts together in an attempt to score.

drop back: when a *quarterback*, after taking the *snap*, takes a few steps backward into an area called the *pocket* to get ready to *pass*.

drop kick: a type of *free kick* where a player drops the ball and kicks it right after it hits the ground; rarely used today.

eligible receiver: a player allowed by the rules to catch a *forward pass*; all offensive players are eligible, except *linemen* (and, in the NFL only, the *quarterback*) who must notify the *referee* if they wish to become eligible and stand at least one yard behind the *line of scrimmage* before the *snap*.

encroachment: when a player (besides the *center*) is in the *neutral zone* and contact occurs prior to the *snap*; a foul punishable by a 5-yard penalty.

end line: the boundary line that runs the width of the *field* along each end.

114

end zone: the area between the *end line* and *goal line* bounded by the *sidelines*, which a team *on offense* tries to enter to score a *touchdown.*

extra point(s): additional point(s) scored by a team after it has scored a *touchdown,* either by a *point-after-touchdown* (1 point) or a *2-point conversion* (2 points); often, a point-after-touchdown is simply called "the extra point."

fair catch: when a *kick returner* decides only to catch a *punt* or *kickoff* and not advance it, protecting himself from being hit by an opponent; he signals for a fair catch by raising one hand in the air and waving it.

field goal: a *place kick* that passes above the *crossbar* and between the *uprights* of the *goalpost,* earning the team that kicked it 3 points.

field position: the location of a team on the field relative to the two *goal lines;* good field position for a team is near its opponent's goal line, while bad field position is close to its own goal line.

first down: the first chance out of 4 that a team on offense has to advance 10 yards *down the field;* as soon as it gains those yards, it earns a new first down.

forward pass: a pass thrown by a team closer to the opponent's *goal line;* a team is allowed to throw only one forward pass per play, and it must be thrown from behind the team's *line of scrimmage.*

forward progress: the location to which a *ball carrier* has advanced the ball, even if he was pushed backwards after getting there.

foul: a violation of the rules by a team or player, punishable by a *penalty.*

franchise: a team; the legal arrangement that establishes ownership of a team.

free agent: a player whose contract with his most recent team has expired, allowing him to sign a new contract with any team that makes him an offer.

free kick: a type of kick taken to start or restart play after a team has scored, with no defenders nearer than 10 yards away; includes a *kickoff* and a kick after a *safety.*

fumble: when a *ball carrier* loses *possession* by dropping the ball or having it knocked away before a play ends; the first player to regain possession of the *loose ball* is said to make the *recovery,* and his team becomes the offense.

goal line: a line drawn across the width of the *field,* 10 yards inside each *end line,* which a team must cross with the ball to score a *touchdown* or a *2-point conversion.*

goalpost: a tall metallic structure that stands at the back of each *end zone;* consists of a *crossbar* and two *uprights* that extend upward from it, supported directly above the *end line* by a base; teams try to kick the ball above the crossbar and between the uprights to score a *field goal* or *point-after-touchdown.*

going for it: when a team facing a *fourth down* decides to try for a new *first down* instead of *punting* or attempting a *field goal;* if it fails, it loses *possession* of the ball.

Hail Mary pass: a long *pass* thrown high into the air in a last-ditch attempt to score a *touchdown* with time running out; aptly named because so few are completed, it does not amount to much more than a prayer.

hand-off: a *running play* where the *quarterback* hands the ball to a *back*.

hang time: the length of time a *punt* is in the air.

Heisman Trophy: an award presented annually by the Downtown Athletic Club of New York to the best college football player in the country.

holding: a *foul* where a player impedes the movement of an opponent by grasping or hooking any part of his body or uniform; punishable by a *penalty* — 10 yards if against the offense, 5 yards (10 yards in college) plus a *first down* if against the defense.

home field advantage: the benefit a team gets by playing games in or near its hometown, due to fan support, familiarity with its surroundings and the lack of required travel.

home game: a game played in a team's own stadium.

in bounds: the region of the *field* inside the *sidelines* and *end lines*.

incomplete pass: a *forward pass* that touches the ground or goes out of bounds before being caught.

intentional grounding: a *foul* called against a *quarterback* who purposely throws an *incomplete forward pass* solely to avoid a *sack*; cannot be called if the pass is thrown from outside the *pocket* and lands near or beyond the *line of scrimmage*.

interception: a pass caught before it hits the ground (or "*picked off*") by a defender whose team immediately gains *possession* of the ball and becomes the offense.

kickoff: when a player kicks a ball from a tee at his own 30-yard line (35 in college) to the opposing team whose players try to advance it the other way; used to start the game, the second *half* and overtime, and to restart play after each score.

lateral: a pass thrown to a teammate backwards from the team's *line of scrimmage* or parallel to it; unlike a *forward pass* (which can be thrown only once per play), players may lateral the ball as often as they want.

line of scrimmage: an imaginary line which no player may cross before the *snap*; each team has its own line of scrimmage, separated by the *neutral zone*.

lineman: a player who starts each play within 1 yard of his *line of scrimmage*.

live ball: a ball becomes live as soon as it is *snapped* or *free kicked* (as in a *kickoff*); opposite of a *dead ball*.

loose ball: a ball that is not in *possession* of either team, such as after a *fumble* or a *kickoff*; it can be recovered by either team.

man-in-motion: a single player on the offense who is permitted to move prior to the *snap*; he may only run parallel to the *line of scrimmage* or diagonally away from it.

midfield: the 50-yard line, which divides the length of the *field* in half.

muff: when a player touches a *kickoff*, *punt* or *fumble* in an unsuccessful attempt to gain *possession*.

necessary line: the imaginary line the offense must cross to achieve a new *first down*.

neutral zone: the region that contains the ball as it sits on the ground before each play; the area between the two *lines of scrimmage*.

neutral-zone infraction: a 5-yard penalty called against the defense when one of its players enters the *neutral zone* before the *snap* which immediately causes an offensive player to move.

NFL (National Football League): the major professional football league in the U.S. with 32 teams; its headquarters are in New York.

NFL Championship: the game held from 1933 through 1965 to decide the champion of professional football; from 1966 to 1969, the winner of this game played the *AFL* Champion to decide the overall champion in a game that became known as the *Super Bowl*; became the *NFC* Championship game in 1970 after the NFL/AFL merger.

nickel defense: when a defense brings in a 5th *defensive back* to replace a *linebacker* on the field, increasing its pass *coverage*.

offending team: the team that committed a *foul*.

offside: when any part of a player's body is beyond his *line of scrimmage* when the ball is *snapped*; a *foul* punishable by a 5-yard *penalty*.

on downs: the term used to describe a team's loss of *possession* if it fails to reach the *necessary line* on a *fourth down* play.

open receiver: a player who has no defender closely *covering* him.

out of bounds: the region of the *field* on or outside the *sidelines* and *end lines*; as soon as a *ball carrier* or the ball itself touches out of bounds, the play is over.

pass defender: a defensive player who *covers* an opposing *receiver*.

pass patterns or pass routes: pre-determined paths *receivers* follow to help the passer quickly locate them so he can more easily get them the ball.

pass protection: *blocking* by offensive players to keep defenders away from the *quarterback* on *passing plays*.

pass rush: a charge by defenders to try to get past *blockers* and *sack* the *quarterback*.

personal foul: a *foul* that might cause injury or exhibits bad sportsmanship; punishable by a 15-yard *penalty*.

picked off: *intercepted*.

pitch-out: a *lateral* tossed from a *quarterback* to a *running back*.

place kick: when a ball held between the ground and another player's finger is kicked; usually is directed at the *goalpost* for a *field goal* or *extra point*.

play: a spurt of action that begins with a *snap* and ends with a *dead* ball.

play clock: a clock displayed above each *end zone* that limits the time teams may take between *plays* to 40 seconds (25 in college); the ball must be *snapped* before the clock runs down to 0.

play-action pass: a *passing play* after the *quarterback* has faked a *hand-off*.

playoffs: the *post-seaso*n tournament, culminating with the *Super Bowl*, that determines the *NFL* Champion.

pocket: the area behind the *offensive line* where the *quarterback* is protected by his *blockers*, between the usual locations on the left and right sides of the line where the *tight end* would position himself.

point-after-touchdown (PAT): a *place kick* taken from the opponent's 2-yard line (3-yard line in college); awarded to a team that has scored a *touchdown*, it is worth 1 point if it goes through the *goalpost*; more commonly referred to as simply the *extra point*.

possession: having control of or holding the football.

previous spot: where the ball was *snapped* to begin the last play.

punt: when a player 10 yards behind the *center* catches a *snap*, lets it drop and kicks it before it hits the ground; an opponent usually tries to catch and advance it the other way.

pylon: a short orange marker at each of the *end zone*'s 4 corners.

quarterback: the leader of a team's offense, he takes the *snap* from the *center* and either hands the ball to a *running back* to run with, *passes* it to a *receiver* or runs with it himself; he also communicates each play to his teammates.

reading the defense: recognition by the *quarterback* of the *defensive formation*; he may then call an *audible* to adjust the offense.

receiver: an offensive player who catches or attempts to catch a *forward pass*.

recovery: gaining or regaining *possession* of a *fumble*.

red shirt: a designation given to a college player who did not play in any games during a particular year due to injury or coach's choice; such a player is permitted to practice with the team during that season and is granted an additional year of eligibility; most often used to describe college freshmen who are held out of games their first year to mature, becoming "red shirt freshmen" in their second or sophomore year of college.

red zone: the imaginary area between the defense's 20-yard line and its *goal line* from which the offense is most likely to score points.

return: the attempt by a player who has just caught an *interception*, punt, or *kickoff* to advance the ball the other way.

roll out: when a *quarterback* runs parallel to the line, looking for a *receiver*.

rookie: a first-year player in the *NFL*.

rush: a *running play*; also, a *pass rush*.

sack: a *tackle* of the *quarterback* behind his *line of scrimmage*.

safety: when a *ball carrier* is *tackled* in his own *end zone* after bringing the ball there under his own power; the defense earns 2 points and receives a *free kick* from the offense's own 20-yard line.

salary cap: a limit on the total amount of money each *NFL* team can spend on player salaries; determined by the labor agreement between players and owners, it is based on a percentage of league gross revenues.

scrambling: evasive movements by a *quarterback* to avoid being *sacked*.

series: the group of 4 *downs* a team has to advance 10 yards.

sideline: the boundary line that runs the length of the *field* along each side; a *ball carrier* or ball that touches or crosses the *sideline* is *out of bounds*.

single-elimination: a tournament where a team is eliminated after one loss.

snap: when the *center*, while facing forward, quickly hands or tosses the ball between his legs to a player standing behind him (usually the *quarterback*) to start each play.

special teams: the group of players who participate in *kicking plays*.

spike: when a player deliberately throws the ball at the ground; used by players to celebrate a *touchdown* or by a *quarterback*, right after he receives the *snap*, to stop the clock.

spiral: a ball passed or kicked with a spin which propels it further with more accuracy; the ball points the same direction throughout its flight.

spot: a location on the field, determined by an *official*, to mark *forward progress* or the place of a *foul*.

stiff arm (or straight arm): a push by a *ball carrier* to ward off a *tackler*.

succeeding spot: where the next play would have started if no *penalty* had been called.

Super Bowl: the championship game of the *NFL*, played between the champions of the *AFC* and *NFC* at a neutral site each January; it is the culmination of the NFL *playoffs*.

tackle: a player position on both the *offensive* and *defensive lines*; there is usually a left and right *offensive tackle*, and a left and right *defensive tackle*; See also *tackling*.

tackling: contacting a *ball carrier* to cause him to touch the ground with any part of his body except his hands or feet, thereby ending the play.

territory: the half of the field a team protects against its opponents.

third-and-long: when the offense faces a third down and is more than a short running play away from a *first down*; usually third-and-5 or greater.

touchback: when a player who gains *possession* of a ball in his own *end zone* kneels to the ground so that the next play starts at his own 20-yard line; also awarded if his opponent kicks or fumbles the ball across the *end line*.

touchdown (TD): when a team crosses the opponent's *goal line* with the ball, catches a pass in the opponent's *end zone*, or recovers a *loose ball* in the opponent's end zone; earns a team 6 points.

turnover: the involuntary loss of *possession* of the ball during a play, either by a *fumble* or by throwing an *interception*.

2-point conversion: when a team that just scored a *touchdown* starts a play at the opponent's 2-yard line (3-yard line in college) and crosses the *goal line* to earn 2 points; when successful, it looks just like a touchdown; introduced to the *NFL* in 1994.

Wild Card: a team that makes the *NFL playoffs* by having one of the 2 best records among non-*division* winners in its *conference*.

winning percentage: the percentage of its games a team has won during a period of time, given by the following formula:

$$\text{Winning Percentage} = \frac{\#\text{wins} + (\#\text{ties}/2)}{\#\text{games played}}$$

yards from scrimmage: yards gained by an offensive player on offensive plays; includes *running* and *passing plays* and excludes *kick returns*, *fumble* returns and *interception* returns.

INDEX

Bolded page numbers indicate a photograph, diagram or table.

OFFICIALS' HAND SIGNALS

TOUCHDOWN, FIELD GOAL-GOOD or EXTRA POINT(S)-GOOD: Arms and hands extended straight above head (see pages 29-31).

SAFETY: Palms of hands placed together above head (see page 31).

PENALTY DECLINED, INCOMPLETE PASS or MISSED FIELD GOAL: Arms crossed and uncrossed at waist level (see pages 21, 30, 51, 54).

FIRST DOWN: Arm pointed in the offensive direction of a team that achieved a *first down* (see page 13).

TIME-OUT: Arms crossed and uncrossed above the head to instruct the timer to stop the *game clock* (see page 27).

TIME-IN: Arm swung in circular motion to instruct the timer to start the game clock.